P9-AQT-672

Parish Liturgy

BASICS

William Belford

Parish Liturgy
BASICS

The Pastoral Press
Beltsville, MD

264.02
Be P

ISBN: 0-912405-96-1

© The Pastoral Press 1992
All Rights Reserved

The Pastoral Press
5640-D Sunnyside Avenue
Beltsville, MD 20705
(301) 474-2226

Printed in the United States of America

Dedicated to the wonderful memory of
Msgr. Paul M. Andrews,
who often told me,
"Your stuff is really good.
You ought to put it in a book for guys like me."

CONTENTS

Of the many thought-provoking insights and suggestions contained in this volume, one which strikes me as particularly challenging is the reminder that many who participate at Mass each Sunday are too young to remember the exciting and challenging days of the liturgical reform which followed the Second Vatican Council. Those of us who were priests at the time found ourselves trying to educate our people to appreciate the beautiful liturgical tradition of the church, renewed by the fathers of the council. Much remains to be done to enable the people of our parishes to recognize the gift of the liturgy of the church—the holy sacrifice of the Mass, the liturgy of the hours, etc.—and also such time-honored devotions as the stations of the cross. All these afford us the opportunity to grow closer to God by celebrating our common faith.

For all who love the liturgy and earnestly desire to share that love with the people, there are many questions which naturally arise in the reality of a parish. Father William Belford, drawing on his wealth of experience after serving as Director of Parish Councils for the Archdiocese of New York and as a member of the Archdiocesan Liturgical Commission, provides pastorally sensitive answers which are easily adapted to the circumstances of an individual parish. Much of what is contained herein reflects the findings of the recent Synod of the Archdiocese of New York, coordinated by the author and successful largely due to his efforts. Attending the sessions of that Synod, I found myself humbled by the genuine burning desire for a deeper knowledge of the liturgy expressed by people throughout the archdiocese. Since that Synod, many parishes have experienced a new sense of the vitality of the church expressed so beautifully in her liturgical life.

Father Belford writes provocatively, so that not everyone will agree with each of his suggestions or his proposed solutions to knotty problems, particularly those emotionally charged challenges confronting individual pastors. To read carefully is to see that Father Belford always gives an authoritative source for his suggestions, and makes clear his own allegiance to church teaching, even in those instances in which he seems to believe that such teaching is itself in need of further explanation.

It is my hope and prayer that those who read Father Belford's comments may find them useful in helping our people continue to grow in faith and so inspire all others to make all that they do each day a prayer of praise to Almighty God.

John Cardinal O'Connor
Archbishop of New York

FOREWORD

For about twenty years the priests and deacons of the Archdiocese of New York have had the advantage of receiving a professional publication called *Clergy Report*—a monthly newsletter edited in the Office for Pastoral Research and Planning.

An integral part of *Clergy Report* has been a column contributed by the Liturgical Commission. I have been the writer and editor of that liturgical piece, called *Focus*, since 1983. This book presents what I believe are some of the more interesting and important parts of those many columns, reshaped into a series of questions and answers.

The articles in this book do not try to cover every issue, but do provide an interesting potpourri of practical liturgical subjects and specific questions which come up in parish life but do not get much attention in weightier tomes. And to substantiate and flesh out my answers, sources from official documents are noted.

In keeping with my goal of providing information to the clergy, my primary audience in writing *Focus* has been priests and deacons. But I also aimed to serve a large readership of liturgy committee members, musicians, religious educators, and others who share responsibility with the clergy for the big ideas and nitty-gritty details that go into making satisfying, inspiring liturgies.

It has been a privilege to write for my fellow priests, who desire to be excellent celebrants, to offer the Mass and sacraments with enthusiasm, to understand for themselves and to teach their people how to participate in awe-inspiring worship. I hope these questions and answers provide some encouragement and guidance for them, and for all the wonderful liturgical ministers who are so needed for great celebrations, and who take their parts with style, skill, and respect for the rules.

I thank my brother priests who over the years have suggested that some of my articles should appear in a more permanent form, so they could look up particular topics when needed. I am honored that The Pastoral Press has made this happen, and I hope that readers will find this book worth using for years to come.

William Belford
St. Catharine's Parish
Blauvelt, New York

INTRODUCTION

1. Why is a liturgy committee important, and what is it supposed to do?

To enhance and improve the liturgical celebrations of a parish, early and continuing input from representative members of the congregation is a major advantage. Not only by making suggestions, but also by sharing the work, a well-established liturgy committee is a significant and valuable part of a parish's life.

As with all groups, this kind of a committee needs to know why it exists and what its parameters are. It needs the satisfaction of getting things done, and the revitalization of regular changes in membership. And for optimum results, it needs the cooperation of the clergy.

Tasks and responsibilities.

A liturgy committee exists to help the people of the parish (or the school or diocese) to pray. We help one another to pray by subtracting the distractions and adding the artistry and polish that encourage people to lift up their hearts in praise.

A liturgy committee is given, and accepts, a high degree of responsibility for the public worship of the community. As with other important matters, ultimate responsibility for worship resides with the pastor, but this committee exists to help him help the community.

Every community, whether it is a family, neighborhood, parish, or nation, has three characteristics:

Characteristics and concerns.

- it offers a sense of identity to its people;
- it elicits a commitment from its people;
- it accepts responsibility for its people.

Think about that for awhile in relation to your own circle. And then you will see that for the dozen or so people who are a parish liturgy committee, the concerns must include:

- continuity for the people who have been and will be "St. John's Parish";
- challenge for the congregation to put their hearts and efforts even more into their worship;
- acceptance of the less-than-ideal nature of community.

For example, a good committee will not take the attitude that they are free to tear down and start from scratch. Neither will they sigh and let aberrations slide without trying to teach a better way. A good committee will bind as many as possible to the church through discussion and compromise, with little or no writing off of any group.

Importance and function of liturgy committee.

1

2. Can you be more specific about responsibilities and schedules?

In the 1970s the job of a parish liturgy committee was easier to define: explain and implement "the new Mass," the "new rite of penance," or whatever. That era is over, and some committees have lost their direction. Others have been eliminated. Even the best want to be sure that they are accomplishing all they are supposed to be doing. So the following priorities may be of help for renewal or review.

Three priorities.

Continuing education. You cannot give what you do not have, and so the continuing education of the committee is essential and fruitful because it is meant to be shared with the parish. There are always other facets of liturgy to explore, a greater synthesis of knowledge and practice to be made. Members of the committee should periodically participate in courses, workshops, and even conventions, and maybe even offer sharing sessions in the parish. Every community needs a leavening group to help the liturgical consciousness keep rising.

Coordination of ministries. More and more the quality of a parish is apparent in its lay liturgical ministers—the readers, ministers of hospitality, eucharistic ministers, servers, musicians, and choir. There is a deep need for ongoing recruitment, training, and coordination of these ministers. Without follow-up, quality and reliability have been known to decline. This is a excellent peer responsibility for the laity.

Creative planning. Wonderful parties do not just happen. Secular liturgies and sacred liturgies need to be planned. The same people (namely, the clergy) who are celebrating Mass and preaching day after day may not be the most innovative or creative when it comes time to look two months ahead to Advent or Lent. Some people with more distance from day-to-day services can help. If there is no group that does this, then what can happen in a parish is that no one does fresh thinking about or has the time/energy/enthusiasm for the special seasons which stir up our liturgical life.

A suggestion.

A suggestion: at the September meeting of the liturgy committee, talk about Thanksgiving and Advent; October—Advent, Christmas; November—Christmas/Epiphany; December—Lent; January—evaluate the Advent/Christmas celebrations and make notes for next year, and keep planning for Lent and Holy Week; February—check up and fine tune and plan for the Easter season; March-April—evaluate the results up to that point and make notes for next Lent, and talk about Pentecost, Corpus Christ, etc.; May

2

Responsibilities of liturgy committee.

2

and whenever else possible—devote to education and ordinary Sunday concerns.

I would suggest from experience that the leader of the liturgy committee be a previously untapped or under-involved person, so that creative ideas and time consuming efforts will not automatically be dismissed as impossible to do. Clergy should be part of the committee, but probably not as the chairperson. I recommend that each member, for essential expertise and continuing education, have and often review Vatican II's Constitution on the Sacred Liturgy and the General Instruction of the Roman Missal. Furthermore, each committee member should have an annual subscription to the *Newsletter* of the Bishops' Committee on the Liturgy. An excellent workbook for group study about the Mass is *The Mystery of Faith: A Study of the Structural Elements of the Order of Mass*.

The *Newsletter* may be ordered from USCC Publishing Services, 3241 Fourth St., NE, Washington, DC 20017. The book may be obtained from the Federation of Diocesan Liturgical Commissions (FDLC), P.O. Box 29039, Washington, DC 20017

3. What is a good strategy for a parish's liturgy committee to follow?

Establish priorities. Set a few reachable goals, accomplish them, and be satisfied. There is a temptation to try to accomplish everything at once. When we try to do everything, we usually accomplish nothing.

Establish priorities.

You could begin by formulating, preferably by group discussion, a short list of priorities. There are many aspects to a parish's public prayer: Sunday worship, daily worship, sacramental celebrations, funeral liturgies, public devotions, the liturgy of the hours, crucial seasons such as Advent and Lent, and the like. The list could go on and on.

Each parish should set a number one priority for a particular year. For example, this could be the year for introducing morning prayer, or the year to get a children's liturgy going, or the year to beautify the sanctuary. Anyone who has tried to do these knows that a year flies by, with disappointing results, if every month brings a new suggestion and unrelated efforts.

Criteria.

What are the criteria for picking a priority? Personal preference or the latest liturgy article should not alone guide the decision. The input of the clergy is very important, but not the sole arbiter, since the whole committee (and parish) needs to be enthusiastic for success. One way to choose might be to ask a series of questions like these: What touches most parishioners? What has true significance for them? What seems to be needed now? What is practical for our parish? What is an outstanding situation that demands attention? What offers a reasonable chance for the committee members to experience satisfaction and success?

3 A strategy for the liturgy committee.

4. How do you go about planning a Mass?

Everyone connected with celebrating a liturgy benefits from an early and orderly review of the many responsibilities and options which are open on a particular occasion. Even a weekday Mass for a few people deserves some prior consideration; planning is absolutely essential when the Mass is for a special purpose that is important to many. Under this description we can include every occurrence from Ring Day Masses to the Easter Vigil.

Especially when people who do not usually make specific decisions about a Mass (e.g., school teachers, DREs, or family members at a baptism Mass, in a wedding party, or at a funeral) need to do so, clergy should be ready to offer them some systematic and detailed help. Such preparation can save time and trouble and assist all to celebrate the Mass in a very satisfactory manner.

Look over the following schema of how to go about planning a Mass, and perhaps reproduce it for your parish's liturgy committee or planners to use.

A checklist.

First Steps

- Before doing anything else, look up the readings.
- Check the presidential prayers.
- Keep in mind the feast/event/reason for that Mass.
- Think of some suitable hymns.

Specific Decisions

- Will we have concelebrants? Deacons? Choir? Organist? Guitarists? Cantor? Servers? Lectors? Special ministers of the eucharist? Ministers of hospitality?
- Do we need a rehearsal for the ministers? If so, when?
- Should the Mass be in more than one language? If so, which parts will be in which language?
- What will be the opening hymn? Will there be a practice beforehand? Who will lead the practice? And from where?
- Who will take part in the procession? In what order, carrying which items, going to which seats? Will incense be used?
- Who will greet the people and/or introduce the theme?

Planning a Mass.

4

- Will holy water be used? Or will there be a penitential rite? If the latter, form A, B, or C? Recited or sung? By whom? From where?
- Which opening prayer? Recited or sung? Who holds the book? Where is it placed after the prayer?
- Who reads which readings? What is the response? Will it be sung or recited? Will there be incense and a procession for the gospel? Who reads the gospel?
- Who preaches? From where? Will silence follow?
- Who will write the petitions, and who reads them? From where?
- Who sets the altar? When will the collection(s) be taken? What will be the music during this time?
- Who will be asked to bring up the gifts? Where will the table with the gifts be located, and what will be on it? Will incense be used?
- Which of the 84 prefaces will be used?
- Which of the 9 eucharistic prayers?
- Which form of the memorial acclamation? Recited or sung? How will the choice of acclamations be indicated?
- Will the doxology be recited or sung? How will the people respond? Will the Lord's Prayer and what follows be recited or sung?
- What extension of the sign of peace is planned? Will there be music of appropriate length?
- Will special ministers of the eucharist be needed? Who will assign them to their places?
- Will communion be given under both species? Who will carry the chalices to the altar? Who will pour from the flagon? Who will distribute hosts to the concelebrants?
- What will be the music during the communion? Who will clear the altar? Will there be a meditative pause? After the prayer, will anyone be making announcements?
- Will a solemn blessing from the sacramentary be used?
- Who processes out? At which point in the hymn? Where do they end the procession?

Musical Choices

When selecting music, pick hymns in accord with the readings; respect the levels of importance given in the document Music in Catholic Worship:
- first, the acclamations: Alleluia; Holy, Holy; memo-

rial acclamation; Great Amen; doxology to the Lord's Prayer;

- next, the processional hymns at the entrance and the communion;
- then, the responsorial psalm;
- the ordinary chants (Lord, have mercy; Glory to God; Lord's Prayer; Lamb of God; profession of faith);
- finally, the "supplementary songs" for the preparation of the gifts, after communion, recessional, and litanies (e.g., Lamb of God and general intercessions).

Be sure to read *Music in Catholic Worship* (Washington, DC: United States Catholic Conference, 1983).

5. How important are music and singing for a Mass?

Certainly one of the greatest influences on the perceived quality of worship in a parish is the presence or absence, and then the excellence or mediocrity, of liturgical music and congregational singing.

Music attracts.

Just as "clothes do not make the person," neither does music make the Mass. But just as clothes give an impression for good or ill, so too the music we encounter in a parish will either attract or discourage. People are not neutral about the art forms they experience, and since we are trying to give people multiple reasons to keep coming to church, good liturgical music, strong congregational singing, and knowledgeable implementation by music directors and clergy of the principles of liturgical music is crucial and in everyone's best interests.

5 **Importance of music and singing.**

6.

How can we improve the singing in our parish?

There is much that could be said here, but I would merely like to pass on some observations made by Sr. Sheila Browne, RSM at a workshop given in Brooklyn a few years ago.

Roles.

• Clergy significantly influence the singing in their parish. The key people encouraging the congregation to sing are: the pastor, the song leader, the organist, and the choir.

• The role of choirs and similar groups is to lead and support the congregation. They also have appropriate moments to sing by themselves. A "choir Mass" does not mean that the choir does all the singing: even there the congregation should be singing most of the time along with the choir.

• Parishes greatly benefit from having someone (e.g., a music director) with vision and responsibility to help people sing at Mass. Priest, organist, whoever: this person's challenge is to help people articulate their faith and come alive at liturgy. He or she should be at staff meetings (and parish council meetings) when parish goals are discussed.

New music.

• New melodies can be introduced during preludes and interludes for a few weeks before starting to teach the words to the people. The best time of the Mass to introduce an unfamiliar hymn is when people are seated and able to concentrate, e.g., at the time of the presentation of the gifts.

Words are important.

• The words of the hymns are very important. Just as presiders need good prayers to say, so song leaders need good words to sing.

People and choir.

• There is no need to choose the choir over the congregation. The choir embellishes and supports the singing of the congregation. There are many hymns and arrangements that provide alternate parts and verses just for the choir, but keep the congregation involved in the singing.

How many verses?

• One way to break down carelessness about singing is to make it a practice to sing at least three verses of a hymn. This encourages people to bother to pick up the book, and gradually convinces them that singing is taken seriously as part of the liturgy.

Good example.

• Just as priests and deacons should be active listeners of God's word, they should give good example by the way they sing out.

Sister Sheila concluded her workshop with a simple sentence that puts some things in perspective: "People don't leave the Mass humming the homily; they go home humming the hymns."

Improving singing.

6

7. Why is a leader of song important?

There are a number of special music ministries. Without intending to slight anyone, a key person who can advance congregational participation—which is a source and summit of liturgical excellence—is the song leader.

Years ago a great musician who created musical settings for the psalms, Père Joseph Gelineau, called the song leader an *animator* for worship. Sr. Sheila approved of that word, and added a few descriptions of her own.

Believe.

- The best song leaders believe the words they sing. They know the power of music; they graciously invite people to join them; they do not overpower the assembly.

Be transparent.

- Like a celebrant or reader, a song leader should be transparent, namely, he or she should not get in the way of people's prayer and participation by displaying objectionable attitudes or habits.

Show respect.

- Good song leaders show respect for the congregation and guarantee that people will not be embarrassed if they do try to sing.
- A song leader may also act as a cantor if the psalm response is being sung.

Be visible.

- A song leader should be visible to the congregation, and should be different from the organist. An invisible organist/singer in the choir loft is not as effective as an organist who plays and a visible singer who leads.

7

Importance of a leader of song.

8. Is the use of recorded music during the liturgy ever permitted?

The Bishops' Committee on the Liturgy stated the general principle that recorded music is "never to be used within the liturgy to replace the congregation, the choir, the organist or other instrumentalists" (no. 60).

Having said that, certain exceptions are allowed: to accompany outdoor processions, in Masses with children, and as an aid to prayer during long periods of silence in a communal celebration of reconciliation. It is never appropriate to use a recorded song to substitute for the community's own singing: for example, we should not play a responsorial psalm and just listen to it. Real people should make real music and do their own singing.

However, the making of real music, because of the non-availability of qualified musicians, is a problem for some parishes. Therefore, while it may not be the most pleasing arrangement, parishes that cannot arrange for musicians should know of the permission granted in the same document: "A prerecorded sound track is sometimes used as a feature of contemporary 'electronic music' composition. When combined with live voices and/or instruments, it is an integral part of the performance and, therefore, is a legitimate use of prerecorded music" (no. 62).

Thus a prerecorded musical setting for hymns might be played to support the singing of the congregation. The great value would be that the congregation is singing, which is better than not singing because of a lack of music to encourage them. But if this option is employed, please do not put the controls in the sanctuary and have the celebrant throw the switches to start the machine. Such responsibility should be someone else's unobtrusive privilege. As with every addendum to our resources, we should preserve as much dignity as possible and do nothing gawky or tacky to counteract the good result we seek. I still remember a Mass where a priest simultaneously elevated the host at the consecration and vigorously kicked a set of bells hidden under the altar.

Liturgical Music Today (Washington, DC: United States Catholic Conference, 1983).

Real people make real music.

Recorded music during the liturgy. 8

9. Do you have any ideas for planning the Ash Wednesday liturgy?

Ash Wednesday is neither Easter nor Christmas, but it is almost as important to the spirituality of some people. We ought to meet them at this point on their journey of faith and truly help them. As we know, this day should provide more than a smudge of ashes. If well done, it will stir up faith and plant the seed of repentance.

Given this popularity, it would seem wise for each parish to implement some strategic plans to channel, enhance, and elevate the allegiance so many people feel for this "holy" day.

Bishops' Committee on the Liturgy
Newsletter, January, 1980.

As the basis for Ash Wednesday planning, I suggest the starting point be some directives given by the Bishops' Committee on the Liturgy.

• The blessing and imposition of ashes ordinarily takes place during the celebration of the eucharist on Ash Wednesday. If the eucharist is not celebrated, the ashes are blessed and distributed within the celebration of a liturgy of the word, using texts and readings of Ash Wednesday, after the homily in the usual way.

• The minister for the blessing of ashes is always a bishop or priest.

• According to a response from the Congregation for Divine Worship (January 1975) other persons may be associated with the bishop or priest in the imposition of ashes, e.g., deacons, special ministers of communion and other lay persons, when there is a true pastoral need.

• Special ministers of communion and deacons may bring the blessed ashes to the sick and those confined to their homes. If a minister is not available, a member of the family or another person may bring blessed ashes to a shut-in, using one of the formulas in the sacramentary to impose the ashes.

Some suggestions.

With these instructions as a framework, and acknowledging the special nature and demands of this day on the time and energy of the parish staff, here are some suggestions to make this day more spiritually satisfying for everyone.

• Preachers should prepare a good, brief homily. This is a teachable moment, a special opportunity to reach the churched and the unchurched as well, who come in part because they can receive ashes even if they cannot receive communion. A story that can grab attention, and which might be repeated at home or at work, is especially good.

9

Planning the Ash Wednesday liturgy.

• Except for stragglers, everyone should be hearing the word of God and a homily before receiving ashes. The proper time for the distribution is after the homily.

• The parish schedule should announce that ashes will be distributed *during* Mass or *during* a service at a specified time. Ashes will have to be distributed after a Mass for those who arrived late, but this is not the ideal.

• Have ministers of hospitality at each door during peak times, with a smile of welcome and information, for example, "We have just begun Mass; ashes will be given out after the homily."

• Make it clear that all who can stay for the entire Mass should remain, that receiving communion is far more important than receiving ashes. But those who have other obligations are free to go after they have received their ashes.

• Use as many people as appropriate so that the giving of ashes can be accomplished promptly. As stated above, special ministers can be used; in fact, any person deemed suitable can be called upon. Choices should be planned; the distributors should be instructed in advance whenever possible. There is no ritual for this. The celebrant first imposes ashes upon the distributors, and then hands them the vessel of ashes, and each goes to a station.

• If the parochial school or released time program will be in session, have one or more services specifically for the children. As with other signs of faith, the sign of the cross with ashes can be misunderstood and ill-appreciated if it is not explained and gracefully given. A sacred setting (i.e., a church) will usually be much more effective for this than a classroom or gym.

As a general rule, especially in busy parishes that attract many extra visitors on this unique day (rivaled for day-long traffic and devotion to secondary symbols only by the earlier feast of St. Blase), parish staff should try to keep the calendar as clear as possible. Meetings, teaching, appointments, etc. should not draw off energy and patience from the main work of the day, which is, by experience, meeting the needs of the crowds which are a gift to us.

If we think, as we should, that it is great to have people in church even occasionally; if we acknowledge that God has been patient with us and that therefore we should be patient with others, then we should make the most of the Ash Wednesday opportunity by welcoming the crowds, and by giving them solid food in the form of the word of God, within the context of a carefully planned service.

Clear the calendar.

10. What would be a priority in our parish's planning for Lent?

A liturgy committee should try to mix creative efforts for special events that draw small numbers with attention to the regular celebrations, when the great majority of the parish is present. Therefore I would focus on the Sunday liturgies.

Sunday liturgy.

For example, one of the first agenda items should be a consideration of what to do differently at the Masses of the Sundays of Lent. What practices will be used (kneeling during the penitential rite or using the rite of blessing and sprinkling each Sunday; eucharistic prayers, e.g., of Reconciliation; final blessings, e.g. of Passion Sunday)? What decorations in the church will be bought or created to proclaim that this is a special time? What motifs will be chosen from the Sunday readings given in the lectionary cycle?

Tend to details.

Lent could also be a special time to address those damaging details that have not been attended to—the sloppiness, the carelessness, the absences that any stranger notices. The institution can show the way to individuals by demonstrating that reform and renewal are possible. I can think of any number of details that turn people off, from flaking paint, missing lights, and filthy rugs, to unreliable ministers, unenthusiastic singing and uninspiring homilies, icy steps that are not salted and parking lots that are not plowed and chilly churches that are not heated on time. Improving some of these would be a worthy first priority for Lent, and a big help for all the other things that are planned.

10

A priority for Lenten planning.

11. How should one go about selecting the readers for the Passion on Palm Sunday and Good Friday?

First, do not leave the assignments to someone who does not know the strengths and weaknesses of every reader. In practice, this may mean that only a staff person who has heard every reader will know whom to select for each role. Diplomacy is important, but for our greatest days we should use our best readers. As a corollary, apportion roles judiciously. It is a shame to waste a very good reader in the "speaker" part, especially if a poor, slow reader is "narrator." The Passion can drag on, the people can become bored, and the natural impact can be squandered by inept lectoring.

Second, keep in mind that:

Divide.

• an appropriate division of labor could be: lector A does the first reading and later takes the "speaker" part; lector B does the second reading and stays in the pulpit to be the "narrator" of the gospel. Finally, Lector A could return to do the prayer of the faithful—unless you need to find a job for Lector C.

• if a deacon is assisting at the Mass, he should take the "narrator" part, and the celebrant the part of Christ.

Practice.

• there is no substitute for practice: all three readers should practice together before Mass to ensure smooth transitions. Specify the choreography and places for reading, who announces the title ("The Passion of Our Lord Jesus Christ according to . . .), whether the words in brackets will be skipped, how long to pause at the death of Jesus, whether and where to kneel, etc.

• slowness does not equal solemnity; in fact, some degree of quickness is helpful to the unfolding story.

12. What can we do to encourage people to attend the great events of the Triduum?

The first thing is to have great celebrations. Personal experience and word of mouth about wonderful, inspiring liturgies will increase attendance year by year.

Another element is advertising. A **bulletin announcement,** like the following, might help stir up additional interest.

For your bulletin.

> You may be among the majority of Catholics who miss out on the greatest events of the whole church year.
> This Holy Week do not be satisfied with just Palm Sunday Mass and an Easter Sunday morning Mass. Instead, plan to be present for each of these unique and inspiring services.
>
> • The Holy Thursday Evening *Mass of the Lord's Supper;*
> • The Good Friday Afternoon *Celebration of the Lord's Passion;*
> • The Holy Saturday Night *Easter Vigil.*
>
> Your personal prayers at home are not enough. You also have to be part of a devout praying community. When people have given these three services a priority in their lives, just once, they eagerly come back to them year after year.
>
> We promise this: your faith in God, your hope in the resurrection, and your love for other saved sinners will probably never be stronger than on Saturday night after the Easter Vigil if you have prayerfully participated in all three of these great events.

12

Encouraging attendance at the Triduum.

13. Why can't there be funeral Masses during the Triduum?

The death of someone we love is always a sensitive time for us; we resent any unnecessary inconvenience or imagined hurt. We want things to be just right. And most of the time the rituals unfold as expected. But there are certain days of the year when most people are surprised to find that what they expected to have—a funeral Mass—is not allowed. The body can be brought to church for special prayers and a liturgy of the word, but by a tradition of the church that is long-standing and of great force, funeral Masses are not allowed on Holy Thursday, Good Friday, and Holy Saturday.

This restriction is not a new law or the result of the Second Vatican Council. Instead, it is part of the church's venerable respect for certain days.

This does not mean that the church doesn't care about what happens to mourners on these days, We do have an approved, official way of praying for the dead and offering consolation to families through public prayer in church. Its form is: greeting at the door of the church, procession, opening prayer, liturgy of the word (as at a funeral Mass), homily, general intercessions, Lord's Prayer, final commendation (as at a funeral Mass), procession from the church. Furthermore, arrangements are to be made for a celebration of Mass for the deceased person as soon as it is permitted, e.g., on Easter Monday or thereafter.

Respect for the Triduum.

The alternative.

Funeral Masses during the Triduum. **13**

14. Why do priests renew their promises at the "chrism Mass"?

This text introduces the chrism Mass in the sacramentary.

This Mass, which the bishop concelebrates with his presbyterium and at which oils are blessed, manifests the communion of the priests with their bishop. It is thus desirable that, if possible, all the priests take part in it and receive communion under both kinds . . . In his homily the bishop should urge the priests to be faithful in fulfilling their office in the Church and should invite them to renew publicly their priestly promises.

Blessing oils.

And yet, from the viewpoint of liturgical history, this emphasis on ministerial priesthood within the chrism Mass introduces a novel element that competes for attention with the original theme. The chrism Mass has historically existed for the purpose of blessing oils, and yet priests are urged to attend this Mass to express their solidarity with their bishop, and to publicly make the "Renewal of Commitment to Priestly Service." Thus the chrism Mass, a unique event for the blessing of sacred oils, becomes the premier annual occasion to thank God for the ministerial priesthood; it is an occasion for priests to reaffirm their commitment to it. Although this is the desire of the church, yet it does seem to overshadow the original purpose of this Mass.

We know that the earliest practice of the church was to bless oils at the Easter Vigil, and then use that oil of the catechumens and the chrism to initiate the new members of the church. Later on, as the vigil became too lengthy and complex, the blessing of oils was shifted to the closest time before the Triduum began, namely, Holy Thursday morning. Eventually the chrism service merged with the evening Mass of the Last Supper. Only in the last twenty years has this Mass taken on the additional character of what some now call a "feast for priests."

A new emphasis.

This move to make the chrism Mass a celebration of priesthood coincided with the end of Vatican II, with increased tensions about clerical celibacy and with many men leaving the priesthood. In this atmosphere, along with a new encouragement for priests to concelebrate Masses, came a special emphasis on doing so on Holy Thursday together with the ceremonies of priestly renewal. For example, in 1969 John Cardinal Wright, president of the Congregation for the Clergy, wrote a letter to the presidents of episcopal conferences in which he stated:

14

Priests renewing promises at "chrism Mass."

To strengthen this spiritual life and consciousness, it is desirable that on Holy Thursday morning every priest, whether he be present at the Mass of Chrism or not, renew the act whereby he dedicated himself to Christ and promised that he would carry out his priestly duties, especially that he would observe sacred celibacy and render obedience to his bishop or religious superior.

When the Missal of Paul VI was published in 1970, the renewals of commitment that had appeared in the previous years were formally incorporated into the sacramentary.

15. May women participate in the washing of the feet on Holy Thursday?

Bishops' Committee on the Liturgy
Newsletter, February, 1987.

A few years back this was a very controversial question in any number of dioceses. The Bishops' Committee on the Liturgy published a short article on the footwashing or *mandatum*. It is worth quoting in full to explain why the answer is yes.

1. The Lord Jesus washed the feet of his disciples at the Last Supper as a sign of the new commandment that Christians should love one another: "Such as my love has been for you, so must your love be for each other. This is how all will know you for my disciples; by your love for one another" (see John 13, 34-35). For centuries the Church has imitated the Lord through the ritual enactment of the new commandment of Jesus Christ in the washing of feet on Holy Thursday.

2. Although this practice had fallen into disuse for a long time in parish celebrations, it was restored in 1955 by Pope Pius XII as part of the general reform of Holy Week. At that time the traditional significance of foot-washing was stated by the Sacred Congregation of Rites in the following words: "Where the washing of feet, to show the Lord's commandment about fraternal charity, is performed in a church according to the rubrics of the restored Ordo of Holy Week, the faithful should be instructed on the profound meaning of this sacred rite and should be taught that it is only proper that they should abound in works of Christian charity on this day."

3. The principal and traditional meaning of the Holy Thursday mandatum, as underscored by the decree of the Congregation, is the biblical injunction of Christian charity: Christ's disciples are to love one another. For this reason, the priest who presides at the Holy Thursday liturgy portrays the biblical scene of the gospel by washing the feet of some of the faithful.

4. Because of the gospel of the mandatum read on Holy Thursday also depicts Jesus as the "Teacher and Lord" who humbly serves his disciples by performing this extraordinary gesture who goes

15 Women and the washing of feet.

beyond the laws of hospitality, the element of humble service has accentuated the celebration of the footwashing rite in the United States over the last decade or more. In this regard, it has become customary in many places to invite both men and women to be participants in this rite in recognition of the service that should be given by all the faithful to the Church and to the world. Thus, in the United States, a variation in the rite developed in which not only charity is signified but also humble service.

5. While this variation may differ from the rubric of the Sacramentary which mentions only men ("viri selecti"), it may nevertheless be said that the intention to emphasize service along with charity in the celebration of the rite is an understandable way of accentuating the evangelical command of the Lord, "who came to serve and not to be served," that all members of the Church must serve one another in love.

6. The liturgy is always an act of ecclesial unity and Christian charity, of which the Holy Thursday footwashing rite is an eminent sign. All should obey the Lord's new commandment to love one another with an abundance of love, especially at this most sacred time of the liturgical year when the Lord's passion, death, and resurrection are remembered and celebrated in the powerful rites of the Triduum.

Secretariat
Bishops' Committee on the Liturgy
16 February 1987

16. How can we help people observe the special character of Good Friday?

Despite the crowds that do come, it seems to me that the importance of Good Friday has been diminished in recent years in the minds of many people, due in part to the inroads of secular society.

Encourage people.

But part of the problem that we can address is that parishes have not provided enough practical encouragement, or religious activities, to really enable people to make this day holy. We should try to reclaim the sacred nature of this day. We could refer to Good Friday more often during Lent, often announce our plans for that day, ask people to be in church on that day, away from distractions. If they have the day off, urge them not to use it for travel or cleaning or recreation; if they are to work, raise the possibility of their objecting to that and taking the day off, as sign and sacrifice. Good Friday is a holy day, a day to be with Jesus and with other believers—we have let this consciousness slip away.

The schedule.

We would do well to start a counter-trend, and see where it brings us in a year or two. People are willing and anxious to come to church several times on special days for good services. A Good Friday schedule could include: Morning Prayer (from the Liturgy of the Hours) in the morning; either a street procession or a three hour meditative service in church, beginning at noon; and 3:00p.m. the Celebration of the Lord's Passion; in the evening, another celebration of the Lord's Passion if needed, or stations of the cross in church.

Obviously, this is not exhaustive. The key element is that the parish staff and/or liturgy planners sit down and talk over the issues involved, and do so well in advance of the day itself.

16 **Helping people observe Good Friday.**

17. What pointers can you give in regard to outdoor processions on Good Friday?

Essentially, you need a route of two miles or less, prior clearance with the police, a loudspeaker, scattered "stations," and a large cross to carry. It can be as cerebral or as symbolic as you think appropriate, with or without costumes.

Not all presiders have enough energy and concentration levels to lead both an outdoor procession and the Celebration of the Lord's Passion. If this is true in your parish, entrust the procession to another person. Scheduling is also important. The people who walked the neighborhood will need time for rest and refreshment before returning to the church for the main liturgical event of the day.

Leaders and schedules.

I have been impressed with the popularity and the ease of arranging a Good Friday procession. It is a definite form of evangelization. The physical activity and the changing settings for prayer evoke powerful emotions. People see their neighborhood and neighbors anew. Beginning in the pews and returning to the church steps for the final station sums up a great deal for people about the parameters of their lives. Some people say nothing and just walk; many attest to a deep feeling that they have been with Christ.

Advantages.

Outdoor processions. 17

18. At what time should the Easter Vigil begin?

A night-time event.

The answer to this question is found in an authoritative and informative document called The General Norms for Liturgical Year and the Roman Calendar, found in the front pages of the sacramentary. This document says: "The Easter Vigil, during the holy night when Christ rose from the dead, ranks as 'the mother of all vigils'." Keeping watch, the Church awaits Christ's resurrection and celebrates it in the sacraments. Accordingly, the entire celebration of this Vigil should take place at night, that is, it should either begin after nightfall or end before the dawn of Sunday" (no. 21).

A relatively new factor to consider is that federal legislation, effective in 1987, changed the start of daylight saving time to 2:00a.m. on the *first* rather than the *last* Saturday of April. Thus when Easter falls in April, we have to be especially careful about selecting the time for beginning the celebration so that it actually be a vigil, so that the celebration starts when it *looks like*, *feels like*, and *is*, night.

Bishops' Committee on the Liturgy *Newsletter* (February, 1987).

While acknowledging the need to respect local consensus, the Bishops' Committee on the Liturgy has made a strong recommendation about the appropriate time for the Easter Vigil. The Committee says that it is dark enough for the celebration of the Vigil about ninety minutes after sunset.

The key here is to appreciate the symbolism involved—the Vigil is a night-time event. It is neither a "sunrise" service nor an anticipated Mass of Easter Sunday. It is a celebration whose motif is that of Christ our Light shining in the darkness.

18

When to begin the Easter Vigil.

19.

Can you suggest any catechetical material about the Easter Vigil?

The following is a short article I have used in the parish bulletin.

> Every year as we get close to Easter, some people wonder if they should go to Mass on Holy Saturday night. They have heard that it takes longer than usual, and they don't really know what this "vigil" part of it means. Some even doubt that it fulfills their Sunday obligation, when in fact it is the Mass of Masses, the holiest celebration of the whole year. So we are publishing this notice for all the people who have some questions about the Easter Vigil or who wonder if it is really right for them.
>
> A "vigil" is a time of watching and waiting for something that is important to us. People keep vigils near a phone when a relative is expecting a baby, or in a hospital lounge while a loved one is undergoing an operation. Vigils are a time of reflection and resolution, of facing reality and making promises. We do what we can to get through vigils: praying, talking, pacing, and the like.
>
> Once every year the whole Catholic Church keeps a special vigil—one that St. Augustine sixteen hundred years ago called "the mother of all vigils." After it becomes dark, Catholic people around the world gather in their churches to watch and wait, to pray and listen, and then, finally, to celebrate the resurrection of Jesus Christ from the dead.
>
> This greatest vigil of the Catholic Church is called the Easter Vigil, which we will celebrate here in our parish at 9:00p.m. on April 2nd. The service will have four major parts, and might take up to two hours. Don't let the extra time discourage you; no knowledgeable Catholic should want to miss the Easter Vigil. Have your supper, put the little ones to bed, take a nap, get dressed up, and then come to church and be ready for a great spiritual experience. You'll be glad you did.

Explaining the Easter Vigil.

19

Here are some of the highlights of the Easter Vigil.

• **A service of light** when all the lights in the church are extinguished and we bless a new fire and light the Easter candle. We pray that the light of Christ, who rose in glory, will dispel the darkness of our hearts and minds. Then we acclaim Jesus as "Christ Our Light" and from the one magnificent Easter candle are lighted all the individual candles held by the participants.

• **A liturgy of the word,** when we listen and respond, sometimes in song, to as many as nine scripture readings—nine of the most significant sections of the Bible. This is a high point of the vigil—we listen for quite awhile to God's story of salvation and marvel at his power and his love. You cannot enjoy this if you are in a hurry or expecting an ordinary Mass. We are keeping a vigil, setting a mood, living a moment of greatness.

• **A liturgy of baptism** when, if we are fortunate, each local church welcomes new members into sacramental life with Christ. It should be the hope of every community and the goal of every evangelization program to have catechumens and candidates for initiation on Holy Saturday night. After newcomers are baptized and confirmed, all of us already in the church renew our baptismal vows.

• **A liturgy of the eucharist** in which we offer thanks and praise to God our Father through the Lord Jesus Christ with the help of the Holy Spirit. By now we are on familiar ground, and yet the words have a richer meaning for us who have been thinking and praying in vigil. The highlight of this part and of the whole service is when each member of the church who is in love with Christ and living Christ's way comes forward to receive the Lord Jesus in holy communion.

20. What are the advantages and disadvantages of having pageants at Christmas Eve Masses?

There appears to be a trend toward introducing religious pageants dramatizing the birth of Christ at "Family" or "Children's" Masses on Christmas Eve.

Some cautions are needed here because it is possible that important liturgical values, and even requirements, can be sacrificed in the effort to make this popular Mass a setting for a children's production.

It is a question of priorities. For example, should a pageant, including Gospel readings by children, sacred songs, and movement of characters, completely replace the assigned reading of the Gospel by a deacon or priest? Should the homily be omitted, with this omission justified on the grounds that the dramatization is sufficient or has taken all the available time? If we know the theology and power of preaching, we believe that no Mass should be without a homily, and certainly not on Christmas—a rare and crucial night for some people to be in touch with the church.

Priorities.

Besides theory, there are the perils of practice: homemade scripts; inexperienced speakers who cannot be heard; intimidated actors in a big church; poor sight-lines with Mary and Joseph unable to be seen. We have all heard people politely praise a show that was objectively awful, just because they want to be kind. That type of tainted approval can creep in here. Who wants to be against children and the Christmas story on Christmas Eve?

Perils.

There are positives, of course, about having a dramatization: the story lends itself to action; people remember better what they see than what they just heard; children are wonderful to watch; some people will come just to see their kids; the participants will remember this happily for years to come; dramas in church are certainly nothing new.

Positives.

So a pageant has much to recommend it. But there are legitimate questions that must be considered: should it be done at Mass? If so, at this Mass? If so, at what part of Mass? Perhaps it could take place before Mass begins. Or perhaps the children could enact the Gospel as it is read by the deacon or priest. Or maybe the pageant could precede the final blessing, with the participants taking part in the recessional procession.

Questions.

Talented people on the local scene will be the ones to make such choices. But priorities should not get reversed: any dramatizations should fit into and enhance the Mass, and not vice-versa. People should hear the Gospel competently proclaimed and applied in a homily that encourages and challenges them; and they

Christmas Eve pageants.

20

should participate in a religious service that does not get overshadowed by a children's show. If I come to ooh and aah at lovely, talented children performing a play, I may be inspired to praise their Creator a few minutes later—or I may be tired of the larger event once the children's show is over.

You can detect my concern here. Perhaps it is misplaced. But there are questions to be considered before we slip into a new practice.

21. Do you have any more thoughts about pageants on Christmas Eve?

Well, I certainly received a lot of reaction when what I wrote above first appeared in *Focus*. Several people mentioned their own negative experiences with this and were happy that someone else was voicing reservations.

And yet a vote in favor of the practice came from a different cultural experience than my own. A priest in a Hispanic parish noted that while Hispanics do not usually come to Christmas Mass in large numbers, scheduling a children's pageant did bring many parishioners to Christmas Eve Mass.

My concern was at first theoretical, but it turned out to be a good preparation for reality once I was appointed pastor of a suburban parish. This parish had a tradition of a Christmas Eve pageant at the early evening Mass. The year before I arrived, eighty children performed at this Mass, which would be packed to the doors anyway; it was uncomfortable and unwieldy, and every value of prayer and performance suffered as a result.

With some trepidation, the associate pastor and I met with the parish liturgy committee, showed them my article about conflicting values and priorities, and offered a new possibility. They were aware of the problems and agreeable to a change.

As a result, we created a new parish event for the week before Christmas: a Children's Christmas Pageant in church and a ceremonial Tree Lighting outside, followed by refreshments. The prayer service in church was a liturgy of the word combining five brief readings from the Old Testament prophets with a modified dramatization of the birth of Christ.

This compromise met the interests of the many parents with children in public schools who wanted their children to experience the religious essence of Christmas, via the dramatic staging and hymn singing and costuming that the public schools no longer provide. It also met our liturgical concern about separating this pageant from the Christmas Eve Mass, and allowing other planning to make that an excellent experience.

Liturgical purists may see this as a compromise, because we are sponsoring a Christmas pageant in church during Advent, but it is not a Mass and we are incorporating Advent themes. And it remains clear that everyone should come back for the great celebration on Christmas itself.

A compromise solution.

More thoughts about Christmas Eve pageants. 21

22. What can our parish do to improve the celebration of Mass on Holy Days of Obligation?

Clergy and liturgy committee members could consider a few ideas like these:

Educate.
• start to educate people about the essence of these days—that they are special days, like Sundays, for attending Mass and for refraining from servile work if possible—and about the meaning and importance of each day as it occurs;

Evaluate.
• be open in evaluating people's needs vis-à-vis the ministers. Putting the right priest on for a particular Mass is always important, and especially on these days. Fairness and equality of work are to be considered. but assigning the slowest priest to the noonday Mass, or the least fluent priest to the Mass with the largest crowd cannot be in the best interests of the people;

Ask.
• ask the song leaders and musicians for their input and their presence and be willing to pay them as needed, so that holy day Masses are not perceived as second class celebrations;

Recruit.
• actively recruit a core of people who can come every holy day to be readers, eucharistic ministers, ushers, servers, etc.

Advertise.
• advertise these days in a better manner, with clear pulpit announcements every preceding Sunday, with signs and handouts so that the people know that such a day is about to occur;

Reach out.
• reach out to the neighborhood and help workers in the area to know the schedule of daytime Masses;

Teach.
• teach clearly that coming to Mass on these days continues to be an obligation, but also relieve those who are afraid of sinning by saying clearly that circumstances can excuse them from this obligation, and that under those circumstances there is no danger of them committing serious sin if they have to miss Mass.

Any event that brings people to church is an opportunity to help them love the Lord and uplift their hearts. The greatest proof of our commitment to the people's needs and of the importance of these days for our Catholic character will be shown by our efforts to make every holy day Mass as prayerful and as inspiring as it can be.

22

Improving Holy Day celebrations.

23. I have heard about a special collection of Masses in honor of the Blessed Virgin. What is this about?

Since Vatican II some new Mass formularies in honor of the Blessed Virgin have been composed, and others have been revised. The approved Latin book containing these Mass has forty-six Mass formularies. Twelve have been approved and released for publication in a volume entitled *Collection of Masses of the Blessed Virgin Mary*.

As with just about every post-Vatican II book intended for liturgical usage, there is a wealth of valuable information given in the official introduction to the book. For example, it sets the stage for our appreciation of the many reasons why the church reveres Mary, e.g., as the New Eve, as Mother, as Disciple of Christ, etc.

Emphasis is given to the fact that the correct use of this *Collection* requires full respect for the seasons of the liturgical year. Each of the twelve Masses identifies with a liturgical season. In Advent there is a Mass called "The Visitation of the Blessed Virgin Mary"; for the Christmas season, "Holy Mary, Mother of God." The Marian Mass for the Lenten season is "The Blessed Virgin Mary at the Foot of the Cross"; and during Eastertime, "The Blessed Virgin Mary, Queen of Apostles."

The titles of the other Masses in this volume, all recommended for use during Ordinary Time, are: "The Blessed Virgin Mary . . .

- Seat of Wisdom
- Image and Mother of the Church
- Queen of All Creation
- Mother of Good Counsel
- Cause of Our Joy
- Mother of Divine Hope
- Health of the Sick
- Queen of Peace

Each Mass offers at least one opening prayer, a prayer over the gifts, a preface, and a prayer after communion.

Appropriate scripture readings for each Mass are given in the second part of the book. However, during the seasons of Advent, Christmas, Lent, and Easter the readings are those assigned for the day in the seasonal lectionary. During ordinary time the priest should consult with others to determine whether the readings of the day or those contained in this volume would be more beneficial.

This volume is available from the Catholic Book Publishing Company, 257 W. 17th St., New York, NY 10011.

Respect the seasons.

24. What is the purpose of celebrating a Mass on Saturday in honor of the Blessed Virgin?

The Introduction (nos. 35-36) to the *Collection of Masses of the Blessed Virgin* explains the history and rationale for this practice.

> The custom of dedicating Saturday to the Blessed Virgin Mary arose in Carolingian monasteries at the end of the 8th century and soon spread throughout Europe. The custom also was incorporated into liturgical books of the local Churches and became part of the heritage of the religious orders of evangelical and apostolic life that were founded early in the 13th century.

> In the liturgical reform following the Council of Trent, the custom of celebrating a memorial of the Blessed Virgin Mary on Saturday was incorporated into the Missale Romanum.

> The liturgical reform of the Second Vatican Council clarified the meaning of the memorial of the Blessed Virgin on Saturday and gave it new vigor by making possible a more frequent celebration of this memorial, increasing the number of formularies and biblical readings, and revising the euchological texts.

> A number of ecclesial communities celebrate the memorial of the Blessed Virgin on Saturday as a kind of introduction to the Lord's Day. As they prepare to celebrate the weekly remembrance of the Lord's resurrection, these communities look with great reverence to the Blessed Virgin, who alone of all his disciples, on that 'great Sabbath' when Christ lay in the tomb, kept watch with full faith and hope and awaited his resurrection.

> This 'ancient and . . . as it were, humble memorial' of Mary recurring each week is in a certain way a reminder of the unfailing presence of the Blessed Virgin in the life of the Church.

25. What happens when the Feast of St. Blase falls on a Sunday and the people want their throats blessed?

Obviously the celebration of Sunday takes precedence over an optional memorial like the Feast of St. Blase, and the prayers and readings of Sunday have to be used. According to the official document: "Because of its special importance, the celebration of Sunday is replaced only by solemnities or by feasts of the Lord. The Sundays of Advent, Lent, or the Easter season, however, take precedence over all solemnities and feasts of the Lord. Solemnities that occur on these Sundays are observed on the preceding Saturday."

Even though the Mass has to be of the Sunday, the saint could be mentioned in the homily, general intercessions, and/or the eucharistic prayer. Then, depending on the size of the congregation and the number of ministers, you might decide to offer individual blessings after some or all of the Masses, or during another service at another time, for example, at evening prayer. Or you could give a general blessing to everyone at once, for example, at the end of the homily or at the end of Mass.

Another option is to offer the Mass of St. Blase on another day when it does not interfere with another feast. This could be done in accord with the following directive: "On weekdays of ordinary time, the priest may choose the weekday Mass, the Mass of an optional memorial, the Mass of a saint listed in the martyrology for that day, a Mass for various occasions, or a votive Mass."

At that Mass the blessing of throats could be given, because this act is a sacramental, and as such can be celebrated at any time. (We may not want to broadcast the fact, but the blessing of throats can be given year 'round.) Thus there is another legitimate liturgical possibility to respect devotional desires and to avoid unhappiness on the part of people who have a deep love for this (or on another occasion, for another sacramental) and who do not understand why, in effect, "our priests won't allow it this year" or "the priests don't want to do it just because it is Sunday."

General Norms for the Liturgical Year and Calendar, no. 5.

The Feast of St. Blase falling on Sunday.

25

26. What are some criteria for readers?

Readers share with homilists the challenging and sometimes daunting responsibility of holding a congregation's attention. Twentieth-century American people do not ordinarily just sit still and listen to any individual for minutes at a time. What we try to do in the liturgy of the word is extraordinary in audacity but also in importance.

Let us recall how crucial the spoken word is:

Constitution on the Sacred Liturgy, no. 24.

> Sacred Scripture is of paramount importance in the celebration of the liturgy. It is from Scripture that lessons are read and explained in the homily, and psalms are sung; the prayers, collects, and liturgical songs are scriptural in their inspiration and it is from Scripture that actions and signs deserve their meaning. Thus if the restoration, progress, and adaptation of the sacred liturgy are to be achieved, it is necessary to promote that warm and living love for Scripture to which the venerable tradition of both Eastern and Western rites gives testimony.

This is the theory; and it is supported by practice. The more people know about the Bible, the better they respond to the readings. The more a reader is perceived as boring, the more the reader's message is summarily dismissed. This holds true even if the reader is ordained.

26

Criteria for readers.

27. What are the virtues of an excellent reader?

The following would include what I would call the *virtues* of a great reader:

- practices aloud beforehand;
- is dependable and ready ten minutes before Mass begins;
- checks to see where the readings are in the lectionary;
- walks with dignity, bows or genuflects with grace;
- reads from the lectionary and not from a folded over missalette;
- looks at the congregation while saying distinctly "A reading . . .";
- conveys enthusiasm and understanding of the reading;
- concludes with a head-up, non-apologetic "The word of the Lord."
- reads the petitions as if he or she wrote them;
- is 100 percent correct on the pronunciation of every name;
- reads announcements and letters with dispatch.

It seems to me that the liturgically ideal reader will do three things very well: (1) take his or her part confidently in the total celebration; (2) make difficult passages easier for the congregation to grasp; and (3) approach the listeners with a subtle sense of "Say, I've got something to share with you . . ."

28. Can girls serve at Mass?

There aren't too many hot potatoes left in the liturgical field, but this is certainly one of them. Both laity and clergy have strong opinions on this matter. There are those, in both groups, who either abhor or delight in female servers. Law and logic are not in love on this subject, and it might be helpful for us to know that some parishes have found a peaceful middle ground.

The problem.
First, the polarities. Rome still says that only boys should serve at the altar. And yet, as people point out, women can read, play music and sing, even distribute communion. So why can't girls serve?

Like every cause, this can become celebrated. Resentments arise, and the question is never really laid to rest. A priest, deacon, or liturgy committee member may find precious little to say after "The pope is against it" or "The law does not allow it." Truthfully, the "why" on this question is weak; present permissions for women to participate in other nonordained ministries at liturgy leave this one prohibition on solitary ground.

A solution.
Some parishes have decided not to follow this rule at all; others have tried to be both "orthodox" and flexible, making a legal distinction about "the altar" and establishing a pattern of compromise. Boys and girls are assigned together: the girls carry candles in the processions, receive the gifts, and have assigned places in the sanctuary. Their duties are differentiated from those of the boys, who are the one to actually assist the priest at the altar.

This procedure observes the letter of the law since the girls do not go to the altar; and yet it provides them a fairly equal opportunity to share the ministry of serving at Mass. There is no organizational conflict between the boys and girls, no loss of servers or slacking off of quality on this account. If anything, the complementarity of roles seems to enhance the liturgy. Furthermore, a source of resentment has been resolved.

Exactly how many parishes have female servers is not a statistic found in the Annual Sacramental Report, but such communities do exist. In any case, all who serve at Mass, both boys and girls, should receive proper formation to do so.

28 Girls serving at Mass.

29. Should a priest or a layperson be placed in charge of the servers?

Traditionally, being in charge of the altar boys was a task delegated by the pastor to one of his associates. But many of the jobs that priests did in decades past are now coming under necessary review. Experience is showing that the clergy cannot meet every demand. Priests have many things to do, including many that have nothing to do with being ordained.

Altar servers are a perfect example of this. The liturgy has a place for servers and is enhanced by good servers. It does not seem right, from the perspectives of theory or practice, for clergy to eliminate servers—or to be so busy that they fail to recruit or instruct them. It is much better to delegate the responsibility than to just let a need lie fallow if they cannot do it well themselves.

This takes nothing away from the priest. If a priest (or deacon) has great rapport with youth and loves being the director of the servers, good for him. But if a priest has no enthusiasm or time or skill for shaping up new helpers, let him find a talented and interested person, teach that person what to teach, and then let him or her be responsible for the altar servers.

30. When did we start to have special ministers of the eucharist?

The practice of having lay persons help the clergy distribute the eucharist goes back to the papal document *Immensae Caritatis* issued on 29 January 1973. The key text said: "Provision must be made lest reception of communion become impossible or difficult owing to a lack of a sufficient number of ministers." The newly authorized special ministers would assist or substitute for the ordinary ministers "in cases of genuine need." These situations were specified as follows:

"Genuine need."

- whenever there is no priest, deacon, or acolyte;
- whenever these are prevented from administering holy communion because of another pastoral ministry or because of ill health or advanced age;
- whenever the number of the faithful requesting holy communion is such that the celebration of Mass, or the distribution of holy communion outside of Mass, would be unduly prolonged.

Besides assisting with the distribution of the eucharistic bread at many Masses, the use of these special ministers of the eucharist has proven very effective in regard to the administration of the eucharistic cup at Mass and in taking communion to the homebound.

Document after document since the Second Vatican Council has been in favor of the laity receiving communion under both kinds. Practical difficulties in implementing this practice at all times may exist, but one of them should not be the lack of persons to present the cup to the communicants.

Bringing the eucharist to the homebound, especially on Sundays, should be a priority of every parish. Having trained and dedicated special eucharistic ministers makes this possible.

30 **Origin of special eucharistic ministers.**

31.

What are some considerations to help special ministers of the eucharist renew their service?

The following might serve as a preliminary checklist.

- Do you arrive early enough to say some prayers in church before meeting the other ministers?
- Does your dress and grooming indicate to you and others that what you are doing is important?
- If you are part of the entrance procession, do you process with dignity or just amble down the aisle?
- After a brief exchange of the sign of peace, do you move promptly to the altar or are you a visual distraction during the breaking of the bread?
- Do you take the initiative if something needs to be done?
- Does it look like you know where you are going? Or is there confusion among the ministers?
- Are the words you speak to each communicant clear and not said in a monotone?
- Are the remaining hosts combined with the other vessels and cleared in a reverent and non-distracting way?
- Is the Mass delayed or are people distracted by your movements or conversations in the sacristy?
- Are you still conscious of your privilege and responsibility?

Helping special eucharistic ministers. 31

32. Why should the eucharist be taken to the sick on Sunday?

On Sunday Christ's faithful must gather together. We must continue to become the Body of Christ by partaking of his body and blood. This imperative does not disappear when a person becomes incapacitated. Certainly the obligation from law is lifted, but the birthright of our baptism and the hunger of our hearts should never be dismissed. The physically sick need to receive the eucharist every Sunday just as do the healthy.

Perhaps we have not always acknowledged this need. Certainly we can remember the days when many church-goers did not receive the eucharist at Mass. If that were our only experience, one could not be blamed for thinking that the homebound have no need to receive.

But now that the church encourages all in good standing to come forward at every Mass to receive, have we re-thought our responsibility to the homebound? We have been in transition: from practically none of the sick ever receiving on Sunday, to having a regular few lucky and/or outspoken ones—but they are only a fraction of the potential pool. Now we ought to complete the mind-change; to remind ourselves and teach others that within reason, all Catholic people, healthy or ill, should receive the eucharist on the Lord's Day.

Educate.

How do we accomplish this? The first step is to try again to educate the whole parish about the importance of being at and receiving the eucharist on Sunday. Given present cultural attitudes, we must fight the tide if we are to convince people that Sunday and eucharist go together. I once had a pastor who kept reminding the people that "Sunday isn't Sunday without Mass and macaroni." Making a connection in a humorous way surely gets the point across in a very vivid way.

Take action.

Next, we must put flesh on the statement that Sunday and eucharist (intentionally used for both the Mass and the sacrament) go together. We often shoot ourselves in the feet by condoning non-essential practices—like extra Saturday night Masses or Sunday morning sports programs—that make it easy to compromise or deny our primary principle that Mass is the first priority for Sunday. Such situations should be re-evaluated, and priorities explained to the parish once again.

But making rules for others to obey is not enough. Actions always speak louder than words. It is helpful to make a parish commitment that everyone knows about. For example: "St. Catherine's Parish pledges that by the beginning of Advent, a member of our community will bring the eucharist to each parishioner who is ill on a Sunday and who wants to receive the eucharist."

There is another reason for this proclamation. The sick have often experienced this hunger without expressing it. Instead of letting this pledge sound like an overly pious statement, convince people that they are perfectly right to ask for a minister who will bring them the eucharist. Say it publicly and often: "If you cannot come to the assembly on Sunday, the Lord will come to you, in his sacrament and in his minister."

What we are dealing with here is a challenge to our self-understanding as a eucharistic people. Are we eucharistic enough? Or have we failed to implement the permissions—to accept the freedoms—of the liturgical reform that do enable clergy and special ministers to bring the eucharist to homebound people much more often than we used to expect? First Friday of the month communion calls have been a familiar model of pastoral ministry to the sick. Regular visits by the clergy should continue. But they ought to be outnumbered by Sunday visits from a friend, relative, or fellow parishioner who brings the incomparable gift of the Lord Jesus in the eucharist—and also the greetings and prayers of the whole Sunday community, of which the sick are a part.

A challenge to ourselves.

A parish must first preach and write about the connection between Sunday and the eucharist for every Catholic's health. A parish must give itself lead time to build up the necessary number of special ministers of the eucharist. A parish must entrust this ministry to those who are not already overly committed. A parish must believe in the wonderful potential of this ministry to help the sick and to evangelize their families and neighbors. Then and only then will a parish make this pledge work.

33. What should a minister do when visiting a sick person?

The ordinary pattern of prayer—when any minister, ordained or lay, visits a sick person without bringing the eucharist—should be:

> greeting;
> reading;
> response;
> prayer;
> blessing.

Scripture as source.

Scripture should be the primary source for all these. And the sick person can also minister to the visitor: depending on circumstances, the sick person might read the Scriptures, contribute to the petitions, say a prayer for the visitor, etc.

Priests and deacons should conclude the visit with a blessing, making the sign of the cross over the one who is ill; the priest may lay hands upon the sick person. Other ministers can invoke God's blessing and make the sign of the cross on themselves and then trace it on the sick person's forehead.

While most ministers have had the grace of wonderful relationships with homebound people to whom they brought the eucharist, the reality is that not every encounter is inspiring for the visitor or the one being visited. When we talk about "communion calls," we are dealing with personal chemistries that may not complement one another. Some ministers show compassion easily; others seem remote and cold. Some ministers hurry a visit—in and

Act in a human way.

out in two minutes; others have the willingness to sit and listen to a litany of problems. People pick up on the sincerity, patience, and prayerfulness of a minister, even if they do not express it. Most of us realize that only the Lord knows which is more important to some people, the communion or the communing.

There can also be expectations and experiences that may not be stated and yet may be a cause of upset. For example, a previous minister always phoned first, and the present minister never thinks to do so. Some ministers are very reliable ("faithful" is the way I've heard it put), which is something that people appreciate; others are always changing the day or time to accommodate "other work," which tells the sick where they stand in importance.

The fact is that most ministers can get into a routine with "their" communion calls, a routine that is too casual, perfunctory, or automatic—and this is neither fair to the people nor good for the minister. Those who feel they have fallen into a routine do well to read or re-read chapter three of Pastoral Care of the Sick.

33

Visiting a sick person.

And those who have taken this responsibility should consider passages like the following:

> Priests with pastoral responsibilities should see to it that the sick or aged, even though not seriously ill or in danger of death, are given every opportunity to receive the eucharist frequently, even daily, especially during the Easter season. They may receive communion at any hour. Those who care for the sick receive communion with them, in accord with the usual norms. To provide frequent communion for the sick, it may be necessary to ensure that the community has a sufficient number of ministers of communion . . . (Pastoral Care of the Sick, no. 72).

Avoid routine.

What should a visit bringing holy communion be like? The official documents give four main parts:

Introductory Rites
    Greeting
    Sprinkling
    Penitential Rite
Liturgy of the Word
    Reading
    Response
    General Intercessions
Liturgy of Holy Communion
    Lord's Prayer
    Communion
    Silent Prayer
    Prayer after Communion
Concluding Rite
    Blessing

The structure.

Consult the third chapter of Pastoral Care of the Sick for the variety of options and readings. There is also encouragement—when bringing communion to the sick in hospitals—to do more than say "Body of Christ." A wonderful example is given by special ministers of the eucharist who visit a limited number of patients and actually pray with each one.

A practical commentary is my *Special Ministers of the Eucharist* (NY: Pueblo, 1984, now available from The Liturgical Press).

34. What are ushers supposed to do?

Although most people use the word "usher," there is something to be said for another title like "minister of hospitality" because it accurately describes the kind of service to be given.

Hospitality.

This title, besides being descriptive, has the advantage of creating a clearer, perhaps more attractive, image than the word "usher." After all, people know what hospitality is. Without referring to a dictionary, most don't know that the word usher comes from the Old French word "uisser," a derivation of the Latin "ostiarius," meaning doorkeeper.

Historically, such a person not only guarded the door, but also had the duty of introducing strangers, and of walking in front of persons of rank, leading them to their places. Whereas it might be worthwhile to explain all this, a new title—like minister of hospitality—might describe the job more clearly, attract more interest, and avoid such terms as "usherette."

Without trying to be comprehensive, we can list some of the tasks of a minister of hospitality. He or she:

Some tasks.

- is present or provides a substitute for all assignments;
- arrives early and spends time in private prayer;
- reads in advance the Scriptures for the day (since he or she may be distracted during the liturgy of the word);
- checks the neatness of the church, picks up tissues, papers, etc.
- straightens missalettes or song books;
- is properly attired and groomed;
- stands by an entrance and greets people, especially looking to welcome strangers and making them feel at home, possibly introducing them to others;
- invites and/or gives directions to those who will carry the gifts to the altar;
- seats people at appropriate times once Mass begins;
- does not move around during the readings;
- takes his or her reserved seat in the back as soon as late-comings subside, and continues to participate in the Mass;
- readies the collection baskets, and takes up the collection(s) with kindness and dignity;
- helps, as needed, during the distribution of the eucharist;

- stands near an exit with sufficient bulletins for everyone;
- wishes people a good day and sends them home with a smile;
- checks the church for any valuables left behind.

Clergy should make sure that ministers of hospitality in the parish know what is expected of them. There is a wonderful spirit of pride when people know their jobs, see that they are important, and are enabled to do them well.

35. What are some qualities to look for in a minister of hospitality?

A minister of hospitality should possess the qualities of friendliness, alertness, helpfulness, common sense, and personal spirituality. We might include here a willingness to mop a wet vestibule, to clean up after a person has been sick, or to gently convince a person who is acting inappropriately to leave the church.

A minister should be sympathetic and sensitive, able to take abuse without escalating trouble, and able to handle in a Christ-like way people who sometimes disturb others.

Ministers should see themselves as servants rather than bosses, members of the congregation who have come to pray but will have some unique things to do for others within the Mass.

Ministers should find enjoyment in fulfilling this ministry. Should they become tired of its responsibilities, they should be given a chance to step aside, be thanked for the service they have given, and graciously be offered an opportunity to fulfill another ministry in the parish.

35 Qualities of ministers of hospitality.

36. How can we recruit more ushers or ministers of hospitality?

One strategy would be to invite all present ushers to a party along with their spouses. Ushers or ministers of hospitality function year-round. As a result their service can be overlooked, when in fact it should be rewarded. At this social gathering let them know that the parish will be paying more attention to their ministry and that a meeting will soon be held.

The next step is to announce to the parish that an immediate liturgical priority is to enhance the parish's ministry of hospitality. Make an effort to have all who presently function as ushers attend. And ask for new volunteers, people willing to welcome people to church, to care for physical arrangements and worship aids, to assist in taking up the collection, and to provide assistance in any emergencies that might arise. Priests will probably have to do some personal recruiting.

At the meeting itself thank those who have been serving in this ministry all along, and welcome the new members. Go through the importance of this ministry and your expectations for its revitalization. This is a tightrope: you want to keep those who have been serving, and yet recast their self-image in the new model you present to newcomers. Continuity and consideration of people's feelings is very important; you do not want to alienate and lose your old ushers. But past practices need to be revised, and new people need to feel welcomed and accepted.

And this includes women, who often have more than men an interest in, and perhaps even more affinity for, the ministry of hospitality. The General Instruction of the Roman Missal says (no. 70) that at the discretion of the rector of the church, such services may be entrusted to women. In many parishes this has not been a tradition. But there is a general liturgical principle that people should do all that they are allowed to do at liturgy. It is a principle that should not be overlooked.

A plan.

Women too.

Recruiting ushers.

36

37. How can we give greater assistance to the handicapped in our parish?

A good first step would be to have someone prepare an estimate, perhaps through local schools and agencies, of how many people in your geographical area have handicaps, and what those handicaps are. The totals will probably be a surprise and an inducement to take action on behalf of these people—and their families.

Invite.

Then invite some of those persons with disabilities and their family members to planning sessions to see what the parish can do. This is wisdom itself, and will open eyes to the gifts that handicapped people, and the family members who have grown through both adversity and advocacy, can bring to the rest of the spiritual community.

Actually meeting people with interests and needs, putting a human face on an abstract problem is the best way to motivate one another. Another way is to ask some questions for self-examination such as these:

Some questions.

• Does our parish have handicapped altar servers, readers, ushers, singers, or eucharistic ministers?

• Have we made it possible for people in wheelchairs, on crutches, with guidedogs, to come into the church and be comfortably seated?

• Can people who might suddenly need a bathroom find one, and has it been modified for the use of people in wheelchairs, e.g., with wider doors and handrails?

• Do we make any provision for retarded children in our religious education programs?

• Do we ourselves ever think about how especially important sacramental preparation and celebrations are to those children and their families?

Experience shows that there are certain things that every parish can do to help the many people (not only those with significant disabilities, but also the elderly and the ill) who are not able to see, hear, or walk well:

The Difficulty	The Assistance
Blindness/semi-blindness	Braille or large print worship aids
Deafness/impairment	Sign language accompaniment/ audio enhancing equipment

37

Helping the handicapped.

Need for a wheelchair	Reserved parking for the handicapped
	Entrance ramp close to a drop-off point
	Seats or places without obstruction
	Consideration by communion ministers

We have to remember that "the provision of free access to religious functions for all interested people is a pastoral duty." Second, few physical improvements to a parish could be as popular as the ones noted above, and the money to accomplish them would likely be donated, before or after, by interested and/or grateful parties.

For further ideas, see the *Pastoral Statement of the United States Catholic Bishops on Handicapped People* (Washington, DC: United States Catholic Conference, 1978).

38. Often the priest at Mass is called the "celebrant." Yet I have been taught that the whole assembly "celebrates" Mass. Am I wrong?

No, you are not. We need to do more preaching about the priesthood of the faithful. Too many people still act as if it is the priest's job to celebrate Mass for them, or in their presence. The authentic and traditional answer to your question, "Who celebrates Mass?" is given in the Roman Canon (Eucharistic Prayer I): "We, your people and your ministers . . ."

"We, your people and your ministers . . ."

This is not to deny the essential role of the priest who exercises presidency of the assembly. A democracy requires politicians; a school needs teachers; a liturgical assembly like the Mass requires a priest. The priest stands within the body of believers as one both baptized and ordained and proclaims, for example, after the consecration in the Roman Canon: "Father, we celebrate . . . we recall . . . we offer . . . we pray . . . we receive . . . we ask . . ."

The Eucharistic Prayers of the Roman Rite (New York: Pueblo, 1986).

Fr. Enrico Mazza writes: "In the Roman Canon, which is a model for ecclesiology, the distinction (ministers and people) is mentioned but overcome in this splendid "we" . . . Not one action of the anaphora is assigned strictly to the celebrating "priest"; the entire celebration has a single active subject, namely, "we."

He goes on to assert: "We can legitimately say that the entire Church celebrates the liturgical action. This statement is not a novelty but a doctrine taught from the beginning. The innovation, the doctrine that is alien to the Church's tradition, is the doctrine that the presiding priest alone is celebrant of the eucharistic mystery" (p.76). In a footnote (p. 304) he says that for this reason, the second edition (1975) of the Roman Missal altered the thirty-two passages where the term "celebrant" had been used to either "priest" or "celebrating priest," because the use of "celebrant" had been held over from the rubrics for a private Mass.

38 The whole assembly "celebrates."

39. What can I say to a person who complains that the Mass is boring, that everything is always the same?

Any number of reasons might underlie such a complaint, and whatever practical improvements can be made should be made. But you might try to help that person to have a larger vision by sharing statements like the following.

The first is taken from the Constitution on the Sacred Liturgy (no. 47).

> At the Last Supper, on the night when he was betrayed, our Savior instituted the eucharistic sacrifice of his body and blood. He did this in order to perpetuate the sacrifice of the cross through the centuries until he should come again, and so to entrust to his beloved spouse, the Church, a memorial of his death and resurrection: a sacrament of love, a sign of unity, a bond of charity, a paschal banquet in which Christ is consumed, the mind is filled with grace, and a pledge of future glory is given to us.

The second was penned by Dom Gregory Dix and combines the beauty of simple English prose with Dom Gregory's love for the eucharist.

> At the heart of our life is the eucharistic action, a thing of absolute simplicity; the taking, the blessing, breaking and giving of bread and the taking, blessing, and giving of a cup of wine and water, as these were first done with their new meaning by a young Jew before and after supper with his friends on the night before he died.
>
> Soon it was simplified still further, by leaving out the supper and combining the double grouping before and after it into a single rite. So the fourfold Shape of the Liturgy was found by the end of the first century. He had told his friends to do this henceforth with the new meaning "for the anamnesis" of this, and they have done it always since.
>
> Was ever another command so obeyed? For century after century, spreading slowly to every continent and country and among every race on earth, this action has been done, in every conceivable human

Gregory Dix, *The Shape of the Liturgy* (London: Dacre Press, 1945) 743-744.

Glories of the Mass.

39

circumstance, for every conceivable human need, from infancy and before it to extreme old age and after it, from the pinnacles of earthly greatness to the refuge of fugitives in the caves and dens of the earth.

Men have found no better thing than this to do for kings at their crowning and for criminals going to the scaffold; for armies in triumph or for a bride and groom in a little country church; for the wisdom of a parliament of a mighty nation or for a sick old woman afraid to die; for a schoolboy sitting an examination or for Columbus setting out to discover America; for the famine of whole provinces or for the soul of a dead lover; in thankfulness because my father did not die of pneumonia; for a village headman much tempted to return to fetish because the yams had failed; because the Turk was at the gates of Vienna; for the repentance of Margaret; for the settlement of a strike; for a son for a barren woman; for Captain so-and-so, wounded and prisoner of war; while the lions roared in the nearby amphitheater; on the beach at Dunkirk; while the hiss of scythes in the thick of June grass came faintly through the windows of the church; tremulously, by an old monk on the fiftieth anniversary of his vows; furtively, by an exiled bishop who had hewn timber all day in a prison camp near Murmansk; gorgeously, for the canonization of a saint—one could fill many pages with the reasons why men have done this, and not tell a hundreth part of them.

And best of all, week by week and month by month, on a hundred thousand successive Sundays, faithfully, unfailing, across all the parishes of Christendom, the pastors have done this just to make the *plebs sancta Dei*—the holy common people of God.

     Both these quotations offer much food for thought; both can be effectively incorporated in homilies and bulletins focusing on the reasons for and the greatness of the Mass.

40. What is a Mass "for the people"?

Simply stated, it is a Mass offered every Sunday by the pastor for the people of the parish and not for any other intention. This is one of the fine traditions of the church that we do not sufficiently enhance and publicize. Many parishioners would be very pleased to know that a Mass is offered every Sunday for them but they really haven't heard about it, or at least not lately.

The new Code of Canon Law states: "After he has taken possession of his parish the pastor is obliged to apply Mass for the people entrusted to him each Sunday and holy day of obligation within the diocese; if he is legitimately prevented from this celebration, he is to apply Mass on these same days through another priest or he himself is to apply it on other days" (canon 534).

The Code.

Some priests have found it difficult to fulfill the spirit of this obligation. Perhaps all the Sunday Masses have other intentions, or the other priests have seen this obligation as pertaining just to the pastor and not having impact on them, or no one ever thought to make this a priority. Whatever the reasons, fallback practices are frequently mentioned: offering all these Masses when the pastor has free days, for example, when he goes on vacation, or just meeting the letter of the law by asking some other priest with no connection to the parish to celebrate these Masses. There is even the possibility that the obligation might be forgotten, more through neglect than through malice.

A very positive remedy might be to pre-reserve, at the beginning of the year, one Mass every Sunday and make it known to the people that this Mass is for them. Some parishes already do this, but there might be a further refinement. Instead of always choosing the same Mass for this designation (e.g., the Mass at which the choir participates), why not have the Saturday evening Mass be for the people one week? Next week it could be the 9:00 Mass. The following week it could be the noon Mass, and so on. Make sure the people know about this in advance. In this way a wonderfully sensible and spiritual practice will be given new luster.

A plan.

Mass "for the people." **40**

41. Why do people give a stipend or contribution for Mass?

The *New Catholic Encyclopedia* defines a stipend as an "offering given to a priest, in consideration of which he is obliged to apply the fruits of the Mass for the special intention of the donor." Stipends are a significant part of the financial support for many priests. Salaries paid by the parish or institution are set artificially low, in consideration of expected support to be received by stipends. The non-exact but not inappropriate parallel would be the salary-plus-tip arrangement for those who wait on tables. And as in any such arrangement, discrepancies in remuneration are inevitable: for example, some priests live in parishes which provide a stipend at every Mass, and others do not. Some parishes have kept the requested stipend at five dollars; others recommend ten dollars as the usual stipend for an announced Mass. Some parishes have many baptisms and weddings and funerals; others do not. The net support offered to a priest varies from assignment to assignment.

Some history.

We know that the practice of making a contribution for a religious service predates and extends beyond Christianity. Pagan priests received a fee for their services; Leviticus 2 describes the procedure for making a cereal offering to the Lord, and specifies that after a token has been burnt, the rest belongs to Aaron and his sons. In 1 Corinthians 9:13 St. Paul defended the right of those who serve at the altar to live from it. All through the history of the church priests have been supported in whole or in part by the service-oriented gifts of the people.

In the early centuries of Christianity the faithful brought bread, wine, and other gifts to be used for the Mass. These offerings were used for the support of the clergy and for the poor. At this same period Mass was not ordinarily offered for the special intention of any one person. It was understood as prayer by and for the whole community. The proliferation of private Masses, beginning in the sixth century, brought a change of attitude as well as practice. It is during this period that Masses celebrated for the intentions of the donor became more and more common, although certain councils urged priests not to restrict the application of Masses only to the intentions of those making an offering. Yet by the eleventh century the giving of stipends had become a fairly common practice.

The connection between stipend and intention has continued ever since, and has had a major impact on our theology. Today, however, questions are being raised in regard to this practice as the result of the renewed theologies of eucharist, church, and ministry flowing from the Second Vatican Council.

41

Giving a stipend.

42. What is the basis for this reevaluation of the stipend system?

A number of years ago *Worship* magazine carried two articles about stipends.

In the first of these Fr. M. Francis Mannion traced the historical evidence and the shifts in attitude relating to money and eucharistic celebrations, from the time of the apostle Paul to Pope John Paul II. His bottom line was that our present practice puts us in theoretical and practical trouble.

Contributions have never been unknown or unwelcomed in the church. In fact, Mannion sees the giving of money to the church as a crucial and valuable sign of a person's membership and participation. But our present system of accepting a contribution for a priest to say a Mass for an absent donor, with the priest assigning the fruits of the Mass to such a person, owes more to the Middle Ages than to the early church, more to questionable historical attitudes than to the apostolic practices and ideals. He suggests a return to the Pauline model of contributing: rich and poor bring gifts as they are able, because they are participating members of the community, and from their gifts the poor (including the clergy) are helped. He thinks that a change from our present practice is essential; money interferes with everything else we say about the priesthood of believers and the benefits of the eucharist being for all the faithful.

Mannion suggests three principles for developing our future practice.

• First, that we understand that the eucharist belongs to the church, not to the clergy. "Any practice that appropriates the eucharist to an individual . . . or that suggests the priority of ministerial subjectivity or intention, or that suggests a greater access to eucharistic realities by the one who presides than is available to the eucharistic assembly, offends against the full ecclesial reality of the eucharist."

• Second, that people should be at the Mass and should participate in the liturgy. "The Mass stipend system offends . . . by generating the notion that participation is not the primary consideration, and that one who is absent may actually gain more from the eucharist than those who are present in the assembly but not included in the particular intention of the presiding priest."

• Third, that we need a better appreciation of liturgical order. "The stipend system places a premium on multiplication and repetition, and offends against the liturgy's calendrical and rhythmic nature."

"Stipends and Eucharistic Praxis," *Worship* 57:3 (May 1983) 194-214.

Be sure to read the second article in the same volume: John M. Huels, "Stipends in the New Code of Canon Law" 215-224.

Reevaluating stipends.

42

43. Why is a Mass celebrated by the bishop so important?

The reason is first of all theological: when the bishop, along with his presbyters, deacons, ministers, and the assembly of the faithful, is gathered at the altar, there is the image and reality of the local church at prayer.

The Second Vatican Council already pointed this out:

Constitution on the Sacred Liturgy, no. 41.

> The bishop is to be considered the high priest of his flock. In a certain sense it is from him that the faithful who are under his care derive and maintain their life in Christ. Therefore all should hold in very high esteem the liturgical life of the diocese which centers around the bishop, especially in his cathedral church. Let them be persuaded that the Church reveals herself most clearly when a full complement of God's holy people, united in prayer and in a common liturgical service [especially the eucharist], exercise a thorough and active participation at the very altar where the bishop presides in the company of his priests and other assistants.

Thus our belief is that the bishop is at the very heart of the church because he represents and symbolizes Christ himself. In an era when a bishop's task of spiritual leadership may seemed to be overshadowed by other responsibilities, it is crucial that we pray for our bishops and with them, because in the person of a bishop we should see Christ among us as our shepherd.

43

Mass celebrated by a bishop.

44. Why do we have concelebration? Isn't one priest enough?

The answer here is twofold. First, concelebration, as the Constitution on the Sacred Liturgy states, manifests "the unity of the priesthood." This is especially evident when priests of a diocese gather around their bishop, who is the center of their unity, to celebrate the eucharist. Even when they concelebrate among themselves, this unity of the priesthood is manifested.

Unity of the priesthood.

Second, and more importantly, concelebration is a full sign of the church itself. It is a sign of the unity of the whole people of God. The church is one, and yet it has many members: bishops, priests and ministers, lay women and lay men. It is the unity of the church which is especially expressed in concelebration.

Full sign of the church.

Thus concelebration is not for "ceremonial" reasons, not to add solemnity to a particular feast or occasion. Nor does it exist to "clericalize" the celebration. Rather, it exists as a sign of unity, unity of the priesthood, unity of the whole worshiping community.

Reasons for concelebration. 44

45. Our parish is about to revise its Sunday Mass schedule. Any suggestions?

Many parishes periodically need to reevaluate their Sunday Mass schedules in light of changing numbers of priests and people. How to consolidate Masses without causing consternation? How to explain a new situation of fewer Masses without causing discouragement?

The problem is not new. A number of years ago Pope Paul VI sent a letter to the parishes and basilicas of Rome concerning the unnecessary proliferation of Sunday and holy day liturgies, with the eucharist being celebrated in empty churches.

Cincinnati.

When Cardinal Bernardin of Chicago was the Archbishop of Cincinnati, he published guidelines urging pastors "to examine any Mass which utilizes less than 50 percent of the seating capacity of a church facility," and in consultation with parish leaders "to move in the direction of consolidating liturgies." The goal was to be that Masses would be scheduled to emphasize worship together as a community of believers.

Hartford.

In July 1983 the now deceased Archbishop John Whealon of Hartford concluded an extensive process of consultation with his clergy and lay people by establishing certain norms for Sunday and holy day schedules. Key elements of the new policy, timed to begin six month later, included these points:

- Apart from the first Sunday morning Mass, pastors are to eliminate any scheduled Sunday Mass utilizing less than 50 percent of the seating capacity of the church.
- Each parish may schedule only one Vigil Mass for Sundays or holy days.
- No parish can schedule two Masses at the same hour in different locations on the same property.
- The starting time for Masses must be at least 90 minutes apart.
- No regularly scheduled Sunday Masses are to begin after 12:30p.m.

While these exact rules may not be suitable for every parish, they do give food for thought. As Archbishop Whealon wrote: "Our common hope must be for an effective parish liturgical celebration at every Sunday and Holy Day Mass at which all participate, at which the Mass is truly celebrated by a priest whose strength has not been exhausted, and at which the music, servers, and effective homily all serve God and God's people."

45 **Revising Sunday Mass schedules.**

46. What other issues are involved in reducing the number of Sunday Masses?

Some years ago two articles in *Worship* magazine addressed this issue from different perspectives.

Aelred Tegels deplored the indiscriminate promotion of Saturday evening Masses because this undermines appreciation of Sunday as the Lord's Day. He wrote:

"Chronicle," *Worship* 58:3 (May 1984) 257-259.

> People do not choose to attend Mass on Saturday evening in order to keep Sunday free for reading the Bible and singing spiritual hymns . . . Sunday, for many, is becoming a time of respite from worship.

This is so ironic. Many of us know pious people who attend Mass every morning except the most important one, Sunday, because they came twice on Saturday. Even if the option of satisfying the Sunday obligation at Saturday night Mass is here to stay, we should caution people that they really ought to come on Sunday if they can. (I have preached the centrality of Sunday to the Saturday night crowd with dubious-to-hostile results, but it did open a few eyes and is worthy saying.)

Tegels, a Benedictine monk and at that time editor of *Worship*, also wrote of the ancient ideal of having one eucharist on Sunday for everyone to attend. He says that early Christians seem to have perceived "togetherness" as an essential attribute of worship. To disperse the congregation as we have had to do and have grown accustomed to doing, is really a disadvantage and a violation of the integrity of worship. If in some places we are in an era of smaller congregations, we can take advantage of that to maximize our quality. As Tegels says, "People may think that they are being nicely accommodated with the full schedule of weekend Masses but in reality they are being cheated."

Something similar was written by Fr. Robert Hovda. His article has an answer for all objections, even for those suburban pastors with all the Masses jammed to the rafters. It is his contention that our way of making parishes and our forming of liturgical schedules are at enmity with the vision of the church given us by Vatican II, and that in many cases these Mass schedules are just a concession to bad habits which we need to break.

"The Amen Corner" 249-254.

Obviously not a word has been said about convenience here. Liturgically speaking, the "full, active, and conscious participation" called for by the Constitution on the Sacred Liturgy requires that we favor community over convenience. Community is the key ingredient, now often missing, for individuals to really feel that they are becoming church. Just quoting Hovda's last paragraph may help persuade you that this is so.

> Sunday assembly is for the purpose of making a church out of all of us rugged and ragged individualists. The Sunday Mass schedule is to be tailored to bring me together with the others of my faith community. It is *not* tailored to my convenience, my habits, my work schedule, my date book, my recreation, or the way I have privatized the sacrament of love and unity.

47.

On occasion our parish celebrates Mass in both Spanish and English. What language should be used for which part of the Mass?

Given the lingual complexity of many of our larger parishes, such multi-lingual celebrations are becoming more and more frequent.

Several years ago a publication, the result of a joint effort between the Instituto de Liturgia Hispana and the Federation of Diocesan Liturgical Commissions, gave some useful pointers:

- The goal of Masses which blend multiple languages and other cultural expressions is to unite people of shared faith in common prayer around the word and eucharistic table.
- Multi-lingual celebrations may require the moderate use of a commentator at appropriate points, e.g., before the celebration for welcome and instruction, before a scripture reading for brief comment, after communion for announcements.
- The invitation to pray before the opening prayer can be given in all the languages spoken by the people present, followed by the opening prayer itself prayed in just one language. The same principle of using only one language is to be followed in other presidential prayers and the eucharistic prayer.
- One or both readings preceding the gospel should be proclaimed in the language of the majority. However, one may be proclaimed in another language appropriate to those assembled.
- Printed booklets giving translations do not enable active listening. A brief commentary in alternate language(s) might be better.
- The gospel should be announced (and the homily should be preached) in the language of the majority. Portions of the gospel (and homily) should also be announced in other languages.
- People may be invited to recite simultaneously the Creed and the Lord's Prayer in their own languages.
- While all languages should be used in song, the music should foster a sense of unity among all present.

Guidelines for Multi-Lingual Masses (Washington, DC: FDLC, 1986).

Bilingual celebrations.

47

48. How can I, as a presider, convey a sense of reverence when I fulfill my ministry?

The article appeared in the January, 1986 issue of *Notitiae*, the official publication of what was at that time the Congregation for Divine Worship.

A few years ago Fr. Denis Hart of Australia urged a renewed respect for the role of reverence in worship. He made two points: (1) our external reverence can lead us to a deeper personal awareness of Jesus and his saving activity; (2) such reverence helps other worshipers to see Christ as present and active.

While all members of the congregation must help one another to enter a spirit of prayer—to create an atmosphere of reverence—the keynoter in this effort is the presider. A priest who is perceived as "praying the Mass" will inspire others to break through their preoccupations and truly lift up their hearts. Conversely, a priest who lacks apparent reverence does little to inspire others, and in fact, may do little to help himself.

Respect the ritual.

The reverence Fr. Hart speaks of is not evidenced by personal additions to the liturgy, or excessive elaborations of rubrics. For example, because the whole eucharistic prayer is important and integral, a change to a deep whisper for the words of consecration, or a long period of silent adoration between the consecration of the bread and the consecration of the wine, is not truly more reverent in terms of the liturgical reform. Reverence is more truly shown in the total way that presiders proclaim the words and hold the elements and invite the attention of the people.

Respect the people.

Our greatest hopes for reverence go astray if the actual execution of a liturgical event lacks respect for ritual. There is no way for congregants to avoid disappointment if celebrants move and speak and gesture carelessly or awkwardly. Improvement is not hard; sometimes it is just a matter of reminding ourselves of the special demands of public celebration, and sacrificing ourselves to provide what people look for: composure, preparation, attention, devotion.

48 Conveying a sense of reverence.

49.

What about priests who use a missalette rather than the sacramentary? Or a reader who proclaims the reading from a missalette rather than the lectionary?

It is a general principle that all liturgical books should be of such suitable size and dignity as to state nonverbally the importance and significance of their words. This is church teaching, not just a matter of personal preference or a matter of taste. The General Instruction of the Roman Missal says that "the requisites for worship should be truly worthy and beautiful, signs and symbols of heavenly realities" (no. 253). The Introduction to the Lectionary for Mass states that "because of the dignity of the word of God, the books of readings used in the celebration are not to be replaced by other pastoral aids, for examples, by leaflets printed for the faithful's preparation of the readings or for their personal meditation" (no. 37).

You may know priests who want to crucify altar servers for wearing sneakers, or who take a sacristan to task for wrinkled purificators, but who then demean themselves and diminish reverence by folding over a missalette and clutching it as their constant companion on the altar. My plea to them (and to all others concerned) is that we forgo the use of ten-cent booklets when we serve the community in the sanctuary.

A worthy and noble book.

Using the correct book.

49

50. May ministers substitute a bow for a genuflection at Mass?

As more priests and other ministers at Mass—deacons, readers, eucharistic ministers—join the ranks of those who are physically unable to genuflect, they indeed may make such a substitution.

And yet there is the possibility of thinking that we should promote uniformity by having everyone bow rather than genuflect, for example, when passing before the tabernacle.

When able to genuflect, genuflect.

This allows the tail to wag the dog. When unable to genuflect, then bow. But when able to genuflect, then genuflect, following the instructions given in the General Instruction on the Roman Missal:

- "At the altar the priest and ministers make a low bow. If there is a tabernacle containing the blessed sacrament, they genuflect" (no. 84).
- "Three genuflections are made during Mass: after the elevation of the host, after the elevation of the chalice, and before communion."
- "If there is a tabernacle with the blessed sacrament in the sanctuary, a genuflection is made before and after Mass and whenever passing in front of the sacrament" (no. 233).

50 **Substituting signs of reverence.**

51. Why do we have an entrance procession at Mass?

Before answering your question, a bit of history might be in order.

Once the church began to celebrate the eucharist within large buildings, it was natural to utilize the space these structures provided. Since the sacristy was located close to the entrance of the major churches at Rome, the pope, accompanied by a large retinue of ministers, entered the church and solemnly processed from its door to the altar. The precise period when this solemn entrance developed is not known; it is attested for the papal Mass shortly after the beginning of the eighth century. Outside Rome, where there were fewer ministers, the procession was more modest. But as the Mass was gradually linked to the liturgy of the hours for which the clergy were already assembled, sacristies came to be located in proximity to the sanctuary. Consequently, the procession was generally abbreviated or fell into complete disuse. Today it has been restored, usually with the priest and ministers processing from the rear of the church.

The Mystery of Faith
(Washington, DC: FDLC, 1981) 5.

There are two reasons why the procession to the altar has been restored as an ordinary practice in our parishes, especially on Sundays. Perhaps the first of these is that a procession is a better sign of the hierarchically structured nature of the church, since the priest and ministers emerge from the midst of the congregation as they go to the altar, rather than—as in the recent past—with one priest and his servers going to the altar in a short separate route from a relatively private sacristy.

A sign of the church.

Second, processions of themselves are very human and satisfying actions. They are meant to be graceful movements and pleasing displays of our representatives and our symbols. When done well, processions add an impressive tone to the celebration. Music, either vocal or instrumental, should accompany processions. More than for the recessional, song is particularly recommended for the opening procession because the singing of the community serves to create an atmosphere of celebration, to put everyone in a receptive frame of mind, and to unite people as a worshiping community.

A human action.

Why an entrance procession. 51

52. What order is to be observed in the entrance procession?

The answer is found in the General Instruction of the Roman Missal (nos. 82 and 127):

The procession.

> a thurifer, if incense is being used;
> a cross-bearer flanked by candle-bearers;
> other ministers e.g., eucharistic ministers;
> reader(s)
> celebrating priest, accompanied by the deacon

This order can be democratically destroyed by readers walking with special ministers, readers stepping up to walk next to a server, deacons walking with readers, and other permutations.

All ministers should be reminded to do all, but only the things, that are theirs to do, starting with the way they present themselves in the opening procession. The deacon is to accompany the presider; he walks beside the presider. And he is not to be in front of the presider, unless he is carrying the book of the gospels.

As to concelebrations, the same order is observed. If there are several deacons present, they do not mingle with the priests (just as priests do not mingle with the bishops). The church is a hierarchically structured community, and so there should be a separate grouping of deacons in the procession in front of the concelebrants. However, the deacon(s) of the Mass should always have their places next to the main celebrant in the procession and at the chair. Thus the proper seating arrangement in the sanctuary is:

The seating.

Concelebrant—Deacon—Principal Celebrant—Deacon—Concelebrant

Processions are the first and last things congregations see of the ministers. Thus each minister should strive to do them well. Ministers, as it were, are on public display; they give non-verbal messages to all who see them, by their bearing, smiles, appearance of ease or discomfort, joy at going to the altar of God, sharing in the singing, interaction with the other ministers, etc. Many a Mass has been elevated by the appearance in procession of a competent, confident crew—and many a Mass has been sabotaged by a disorderly and bedraggled rush down the aisle.

As Aidan Kavanagh pungently puts it: "The bearing of liturgical ministers must conform to the scale of the space and the ceremony . . . No sensible person would preside or read a lesson at a liturgy in someone's dining room in the same manner as at a

52 Who follows whom.

solemn event in a large church. Great spaces and solemn ceremonies require large gestures, different voices, more complex choreography, even different vesture. One who does not sense such things probably cannot be taught them. One who cannot be taught them might consider serving God in solitude rather than in the assembly as one of its liturgical ministers."

Elements of Rite: A Handbook of Liturgical Style (New York: Pueblo, 1982) 22.

53. Who should be seated in the sanctuary?

There are no hard-and-fast rules about this. The celebrating priest, deacon, servers, readers, eucharistic ministers, cantors, even the whole choir: all these ministers *could* be seated in the sanctuary.

The necessary question is whether it is helpful to the congregation and to the flow of the celebration to have them all there in the sanctuary.

The worship space.

The single most important factor in each individual case will be the worship space. While some principles and preferences are expressed below, any specific answer will be conditioned by the amount of space in the sanctuary and by the arrangement of the altar, pulpit, and chair.

For example, you can position many people in a spacious, wide sanctuary without having them be a distraction to the congregation. But in much smaller spaces, even a few people with their necessary furniture can create visual clutter. You might decide on the basis of relative need: cantors and servers are frequently needed, and so should be close; readers and eucharistic ministers have fewer moments of action, and so could be seated further away.

Logistics are a major factor: you do not want long pauses and undue attention paid to readers or eucharistic ministers who come a distance to their place of service. This can be a definite reason for seating them in the sanctuary rather than in the front pew or elsewhere.

Principles and preferences.

Here are some principles and liturgical preferences to keep in mind:

• the sanctuary should have few if any additional pieces of furniture; extra chairs and kneelers distract from the three main focal points of altar, pulpit, and chair. This becomes an argument for seating ministers within the congregation;

• only the number of priests and deacons who can be seated in the sanctuary with dignity and comfort should be there; additional seating for clergy would be in a front pew;

• the servers and cantors should be in the sanctuary because they are often needed;

• some choose to seat the reader in the sanctuary to minimize movement; but others like the symbolism of the reader coming forth from the congregation;

• ministers should not have to constantly cross the sanctuary;

53

Who sits in the sanctuary.

• even if you have a large sanctuary, if you have several eucharistic ministers, they should probably be in a nearby pew; they are needed only later in the Mass, and can come to the altar during the busy time of the exchange of peace;

• choirs could be near but not in the sanctuary, because they can be a visual distraction and would certainly need many seats.

When asked about who should be seated in the sanctuary, I hesitate and wonder if there might not be a hidden agenda in the question. For example, does one intend to declare the sanctuary as clergy territory and off-limits to the laity? Or is there a presumption that we are all alike, and there shouldn't even be a presider's chair? In both instances, the subtext is wrong and should be addressed. The true theology of worship is that the whole congregation celebrates the Mass, each in his or her proper role. Where exactly all the folks sit is a matter of space and taste more than of liturgical rule.

A hidden agenda?

54. Which of the three penitential forms in the Mass should ordinarily be used?

The answer could depend on the solemnity or the season. Each form of the penitential rite has a value, and all should be used on occasion. Johannes Emminghaus in his excellent book on the Mass writes:

The Eucharist: Essence, Form, Celebration (Collegeville: The Liturgical Press, 1978) 116.

> For penitential seasons, the first penitential act provided in the Missal seems the most appropriate; it allows a pause for the examination of conscience and then contains an explicit confession of sins in the form of a revised Confiteor. A second form of the penitential rite, containing verses from the psalms, is perhaps best suited to Sundays and feastdays, The third variation, with its several versions of a revised Kyrie litany, fuses penitential act and litany . . . and thus lessens the feeling we may have that too many small rites are being packed into the introductory part of the Mass.

Structure.

Each of these forms of the penitential rite has a four part structure: invitation to the community to recall its sins, followed by a short period of silence for an examination of conscience. A prayer for forgiveness follows. While these elements are the same, the variety of words seems to stir up our interest and combat routine. Emminghaus writes: "The Confiteor had largely lost its impact in the old Missal because it had been used in every Mass, even on great feasts such as Easter."

Use all the options.

There are other possibilities for getting into a rut and using only one option. Some time ago, as the principal celebrant of a concelebrated liturgy, I chose Eucharistic Prayer IV. After Mass, a priest remarked that prayer IV had not been used by him or in his presence for years. If we priests remain very oriented to certain options, and unwilling to use others, the people will be deprived of the intended variety of introductory greetings, formulas for the penitential rite, eucharistic prayers, dismissals, blessings, etc. Surely this is a loss for all!

54 Which form of the penitential rite.

55. May we recite the gospel acclamation if it is not sung? Or may we simply omit it?

First, take a look at no. 39 of the General Instruction on the Roman Missal. It says: "If not sung, the Alleluia or the verse before the gospel may be omitted." But this statement must be interpreted in light of subsequent legislation, for example, no. 23 of the 1981 *Ordo Lectionum Missae* which states that the gospel acclamation must be sung.

The Bishops' Committee on the Liturgy explains: "Since the acclamation *must* be sung, it follows that it may not be recited. And since that is true, then it *must* be omitted if it in impossible to sing it. In other words, what has changed through the 1981 legislation is that the *option* of omitting the acclamation has been replaced by the *necessity* of omitting it when it cannot be sung."

What we should realize is that the gospel acclamation is a song to accompany the procession from the chair to the pulpit, and must therefore coincide with it. Depending on the space to be covered and the musical setting for the acclamation, the priest or deacon should move from the chair when the "Alleluia" song begins; by the time it ends, he should be in the pulpit, ready to proclaim the gospel. Anytime we see the gospel reader rooted to his place during the singing of the Alleluia, and processing even part of the way to the pulpit in silence, we know he has made a mistake.

Bishops' Committee on the Liturgy *Newsletter*, October, 1985.

Omitting the gospel acclamation. 55

56. Why do some churches have a book of the gospels? Doesn't the lectionary contain all the readings?

Yes, the lectionary does contain all the readings. But the tradition of both the east and the west has been to set apart one book for the gospel readings.

The gospel: a special reading.

Since it is Christ himself speaking to his people when the gospel is proclaimed at Mass, tradition has surrounded the gospel proclamation with certain signs of solemnity, for example, the use of incense, candles, gestures, a special procession. And whereas the other readings can be proclaimed by anyone with the skill to do so, the gospel proclamation belongs especially to the ministry of the deacon who, in liturgical tradition, is seen as a special representative of Christ.

A special book.

The book of the gospels is to be a special book, in design and ornamentation, by comparison with the lectionary. This does not mean the other readings are to be proclaimed from a shabby paperback or a missalette. Nor does it mean that the lectionary itself should be allowed to fall into a state of disrepair. It is just a hierarchy of values—the book of the gospels is to be an especially noble book.

When a deacon is present, he carries the book of the gospels in procession. When no deacon is present, it is a lector (not the celebrating priest) who carries in the volume. In both cases the book is placed on the altar, with the lectionary being already opened on the ambo. After the second reading, the lectionary is removed from the ambo, and the priest or deacon who will proclaim the gospel brings the book of the gospels to the ambo.

57. Preachers must study the Mass readings beforehand. Should members of the congregation also read the Scriptures for the day before going to Mass?

Experience teaches us that the best way to understand and remember important information is to go over it several times.

Refreshing the memory.

Very often it is just not possible to grasp the whole message the first time we hear it. This is why a student prepares for an important class by reading the material beforehand, why a shopper checks the advertisements in the paper, why a business-man/woman reads the trade journals. Although each of them is familiar with the subject, they all recognize that they will be better off if their memory is refreshed, if they know exactly what they are looking for.

In the same way, because we are no different on Sunday when we go to Mass than on other days when we go to school or to the stores or to work, we cannot expect to immediately grasp the full message of the scripture readings at Mass when we hear them for the first time.

Even a short reading is quite a challenge for a single listening. Granted, we may get most of it. But that is like getting only a percentage of your salary. You deserve, and need, all of it.

We need to prepare ourselves.

When the word of God is proclaimed at Mass, Christ is present and attempting to communicate with us. If we are not prepared to hear, because of a lack of interest or familiarity or for whatever reason, his life-giving and energizing message goes right past us, and we are merely bored.

If this is happening, it is a tragedy for everyone. Priests and deacons have an obligation before God to preach his word, to open up these readings to these people with their particular needs.

But as hard as preachers may try, their degree of success depends on many factors, especially (1) the interest you have in hearing the word; and (2) the preparation you have done to receive its message.

The readings are so important because much of the Mass is planned around them. The prayers, the hymns, the chants, all should reflect and refer to the central themes. The preacher has made himself familiar with these texts: if the congregation is also ready, because of their reference to the Scriptures beforehand, at least two major benefits are immediately obvious:

• the preacher sees that you are with him, and he is encouraged to give careful, spiritual homilies based on the readings, rather than generalized talks (what we call sermons);

Reading the Scriptures beforehand.

57

• regardless of the impact of the homily (since no one is absolutely inspiring every week) you have gotten more out of the liturgy of the word, and so the Mass has meant more to you.

If you habitually feel lost or bored during the first part of the Mass, read from your Bible at home, or come to church early and read from the missalette. Then you are clued in and can be alert to the key words, phrases, and themes of that particular Mass.

You can't live on half your salary, or half the message from the Lord. You need it all.

58. What are the advantages of preaching a homily at every Mass?

There are advantages both for the congregation as well as for the homilist.

For myself, preaching at every Mass has been a constructive discipline, forcing me to pay attention to the word of God. It saves me from the dullness of routine; preparing passages for *this* Mass makes this celebration different from yesterday's or tomorrow's.

The homilist benefit.

It challenges me to engage the congregation in dialogue; if the people have been lost in a fog, I can pull them in to my alertness; if they have been muddled by the message of a difficult passage, I can help dispel part of their confusion.

Daily preaching allows me to be more creative, spontaneous, and even humorous than I might try to be on Sunday with its larger crowd. Daily preaching is a graceful time/place for building up self-confidence as well as skill.

As for the people, a brief daily homily adds a great deal to their appreciation of Mass. In my experience people come to Mass more frequently when the priests (or deacons) of the parish preach everyday. As long as the homily is brief, related to the lives of the people, and as long as we pay attention to the comments and reactions of the people, a daily homily is appreciated.

The people benefit.

Some priests do not attempt a daily homily because they feel that they will have nothing new to say after awhile. Just the opposite is true. Inspiration for preaching on Sunday comes just as quickly—or more so—if there has been daily practice and prayer. Occasionally the well may go dry; but in the long run it will probably give more water if it is constantly primed.

59. I need new ideas for preparing my homilies. Any suggestions?

In preparing homilies, why not be attentive to our buildings, symbols, prayers, and hymns? Rarely is a congregation bored when a preacher, during the homily, refers to words that have just been said or sung, or takes his people on a tour of their church, explaining the theology of a worship space and proudly pointing out the particular glories of their own church building.

Environment.

Especially in our mobile society, many parishioners have never really looked around the church they now worship in. They may never have learned who the statues represent or what the windows picture. People are still interested in many practical things we have long since taken for granted, for example, why the altar rail was taken away. Getting comfortable with our surroundings is an ordinary human desire, and until people explore their liturgical space, they may not feel completely at home there.

Then there are the symbols in the worship space. Explanation and knowledge promote pride and loyalty in a parish and in its heritage. Mention in a homily could be a graceful way to prepare the ground for future improvements. ("There behind the main altar you see our beautiful tabernacle. You probably know that the church recommends that the blessed sacrament be given a place of honor in a chapel of its own, and we have to be thinking about doing that someday.")

Prayers.

Explaining the rationale and the elements of the presidential prayers is entirely acceptable as homiletic material: "The homily is an integral part of the liturgy . . . It should develop some point of the readings or of another text from the Ordinary or from the Proper of the Mass of the day, and taken into account the mystery being celebrated and the needs proper to the listeners" (Constitution on the Sacred Liturgy no. 41).

Hymns.

We should also pay attention to our hymns. People sing with greater enthusiasm when they know the words very well, like what they say, and are acquainted with their history. Often enough, great music arose in perilous times; explaining that background can help people want to really enter into the singing.

One of the realities of life is that what is popular—obvious, well-known, accessible to all—is powerful. Our public buildings, the decorations we employ there, the prayers, and the hymns, all have messages that might need to be occasionally unveiled, lest they be missed by some people and misinterpreted by others. Simply put, we should sometimes preach on what everyone knows.

59 Preparing the homily.

60. Why do we have the general intercessions at Mass?

Liturgical studies show that intercessions are one of the oldest parts of the Mass. Evidence comes from very early writers: Justin Martyr (c.100-c.165), Hippolytus (c.170-c.236), and the Apostolic Constitutions (latter half of the fourth century). Changes did come about, however, and by the fifth century the intercessions were eliminated from their place at the end of the liturgy of the word (except on Good Friday), but some vestige of them remained in the Kyrie at the beginning of the Mass. Now the intercessions have been restored to the eucharist, to the liturgy of the hours, and to other sacramental and liturgical rites.

Some history.

This was one of council's the major reforms. The Constitution on the Sacred Liturgy directed that the rites of the Mass be simplified, and that "elements which, with the passage of time, came to be duplicated, or were added with but little advantage, should be discarded. Where opportunity allows or necessity demands, other elements which have suffered injury through accidents of history are now to be restored to the earlier norm of the holy Fathers" (no. 50). The document specifically called for the restoration of "the common prayer" or "the prayer of the faithful" (no. 53).

The council.

In 1979 the Bishops' Committee on the Liturgy issued a brochure entitled "General Intercessions." If you have it in your files, share it with your liturgy committee. The authors point out that the church is convinced of the timeless value of intercessory prayer. Parish communities can well profit from catechesis on this: the petitions are not a series of wishes and announcements, but rather a list of real needs that we hope the Lord will act upon.

This document is contained in the bound volume of the Bishops' Committee on the Liturgy *Newsletter* (1976-1980).

Just a word on the names given this prayer. It is sometimes called the "prayer of the faithful." In the early church Justin and Hippolytus both stressed that only the baptized—the faithful—could take part in this prayer. Catechumens and others were to be dismissed before these prayers. Since only the faithful could participate, the name "prayer of the faithful" was used.

The name.

But "the prayer *of* the faithful" is not to be understood as "the prayer *for* the faithful." These prayers are never just for ourselves. They are not just for the members of our church. They are for the needs and concerns of the whole church, of the whole world. This is why the preferred title is "general intercessions."

The general intercessions.

61. Who writes the general intercessions, and according to what rules?

Especially for the Sunday eucharist, those who preach and preside have the responsibility to write, or at least help to compose, the intercessions, and to prepare the introduction and concluding prayer.

Roman directives.

The General Instruction of the Roman Missal provides us with some instructions and a format to be followed.

• "In the general intercessions or prayer of the faithful, the people exercise their priestly function by interceding for all mankind. It is appropriate that this prayer be included in all Masses celebrated with a congregation, so that intercessions may be made for the Church, for civil authorities, for those oppressed by various needs, for all mankind, and for the salvation of the world" (no. 45).

• "As a rule the sequence of intentions is
    a) for the needs of the Church;
    b) for public authorities and the salvation of the world;
    c) for those oppressed by any need;
    d) for the local community.

In particular celebrations, such as confirmations, marriages, funerals, etc., the list of intentions may be more closely concerned with the special occasion" (no. 46).

• The priest directs the prayer; with a brief introduction he invites the people to pray; after the intentions he says the concluding prayer. It is desirable that the intentions be announced by the deacon, cantor, or other person. The congregation makes its petition either by a common response after each intention or by silent prayer.

Ideas to keep in mind.

There are four elements in the general intercessions, and each must be respected.

Introduction. This is never a prayer to God. It is always addressed to the people. As to form, it might be a simple call to prayer, a link between the homily and the intercessions, or a simple "Let us pray." Structurally, the introduction is a short bridge between the proclamation of the word and the petitionary response of the people.

61
Writing the general intercessions.

Intentions. These are not prayers in themselves. They are invitations to the community to pray for a particular purpose or person. They should be announced by the deacon or another minister. There should be a clear, familiar concluding formula, such as "Let us pray to the Lord . . ." The people should not have to guess when to respond. The number of intentions should be limited, so as not to weary the assembly and to keep the prayer proportionate to the rest of the liturgy of the word. Ordinarily five or six intentions suffice; more rarely there might be seven or eight.

The brochure from the Bishops' Committee on the Liturgy which I mentioned previously elaborates on the General Instruction and stresses that at least one intention be taken from each of the four categories listed:

- "The needs of the Church: for example, petitions might be for the Pope, the local bishop, all bishops and pastors of the Church, the Church's ministers, the missions, the unity of Christians, vocations to the priesthood and the religious life, etc."
- "Public authorities and the salvation of the world: for example, petitions might be composed for peace and justice, government officials, an end to war, good weather, a good and bountiful harvest, public elections, the solution of socio-economic problems, etc."
- "Those oppressed by any need: for example, intercession might be made for those suffering religious or political persecution, for the unemployed, for the sick and infirm, for prisoners or exiles, for those suffering racial or other injustices, etc."
- "The local community: for example, intercessions might be composed for those absent from the community, for those who are to be baptized or confirmed, ordained or married, for the ministers of the local community, for first communicants, for a mission or week of renewal, etc."

Silence. Before the concluding prayer, the deacon or minister should encourage silent prayer. There is a link with the structure of the readings here. Each reading is hopefully followed by silence; the same should be true of at the end of the intentions.

Concluding prayer. After the intentions, responses, and silence, the presiding priest addresses a prayer to God the Father. It is never addressed to Christ, Mary, or the saints. This prayer sums up the intercessions and should not include new petitions. It concludes with a brief formulation, for example, "through Christ our Lord."

62. Do you have any other suggestions for the general intercessions?

Because preparing and praying the general intercessions is so important, I would like to share with you some further ideas from the Bishops' Committee brochure. They will be most helpful for all who compose intercessions.

• Since the general intercessions are prayers of supplication and petition, it is not correct to compose them in a style which reflects other prayer forms, that is, prayers of thanksgiving, adoration, praise, or penitence . . . Declarations of praise and thanksgiving should not be included in the general intercessions . . .

• The general intercessions should never be didactic, as though they were announcements. Nor should the proposal of intentions ever become partisan or tendentious. The intercessions are not a substitute for the homily. While their style is not homiletic, they may reflect the Word of God . . . but not as a summary of the homily.

• It may not be possible or even desirable in large liturgical assemblies, as it often is in smaller groups, to invite spontaneous and free presentation of petitions and intentions. However, ordinarily some opportunity should be given to the members of the community to submit intentions which may then be formulated or summarized in preparation for worship.

• Genuine necessities, real needs, should be the subject of the petitions for which the community prays. 'Prepackaged' intercessions often fail to meet universal needs. Material prepared months in advance of the date of its use can hardly be expected to be current. Nor can the needs of the local community which makes the prayer ever be met by such material. A worshiping community must be sensitive to both the universal and the particular needs of the Church and the world. Current events should help shape the intercessions for the community.

62 Further suggestions.

63. What is the basis for intercessory prayer?

Fr. John Wright, S.J. once wrote a very insightful article in which he took a panoramic theological view of all intercessory prayer and made the following points about what this type of prayer is and is not. Intercessory prayer

"Praying for Rain," *Church* (Winter, 1987).

- is an expression of our personal relationship with God;
- deepens and intensifies that relationship;
- is always answered in that sense;
- is not a magical formula to control God;
- does not persuade God to do what God is unwilling to do.

Even our desire to pray comes from God's initiative because God encourages us to ask for what we need. Doing so brings us closer to God, and God to us. Thus in a profound way our prayers are always being answered—by our relationship with God being deepened. Beyond that, God may give us the things we have asked for as a concrete expression of the divine relationship to us.

Prayers are always answered.

Not getting what we ask for in prayer is a popular reason for not praying for awhile. Children of all ages are tempted to stop praying when they don't get what they want. Perhaps in connection with additional catechesis on the general intercessions, there should be instruction on the truths and errors of prayer presumptions. A good number of people still approach prayer as being a *quid pro quo*, a "let's make a deal" way of communicating with the Lord. Parish staff, in addition to preparing worthy petitions each week, should better and more often explain why we pray and how we receive God's answers.

Consider sharing with others the conclusion of Fr. Wright's article:

What if?

> It is possible that God's response will not include the particular result [prayed for]. This, for the person of faith, does not mean that God is unconcerned, but that in the longer view God sees that not having that result has, at the least, the potential of deepening more effectively the enduring personal relationship he wishes ultimately to establish. I may pray for rain and no rain may come; but in the situation of drought, people may discover their need for one another and learn to practice a kind of

Intercessory prayer.

sharing and generosity they might not otherwise have known. I pray for the recovery of health for someone I love, but he dies, as all of us must do eventually. The moment of death lies in a special way within the loving providence of God, who calls us to a union of love with himself from which neither death or anything in all creation can separate us (Rom 8:38-39). I believe, then, that the divine refusal to hear my prayer in the way I have formulated it is really a divine granting of what I most profoundly want: eternal union with God for the one for whom I am praying, as well as for myself. Praying for rain or for any other natural event is then altogether appropriate. God will always grant the deeper prayer implicit in my request, the prayer for closer and stronger personal union with him. He may also grant the concrete thing for which I am asking, if indeed it will foster that union more truly than not granting it.

64. Why is it wrong to call the preparation of the gifts the "offertory"?

Several years ago the Bishops' Committee on the Liturgy pointed out that the title "'preparation of the gifts' helps correct the mistaken notion that this is an 'offertory' distinct from or anticipatory of the eucharistic prayer."

The excellent publication *The Mystery of Faith* (p. 62) fills in some historical facts:

> Until the eleventh century, the Roman Mass knew only one prayer during the preparation rite, i.e., the prayer said over the gifts immediately before the eucharistic prayer. But once the procession with the gifts began to disappear, various prayers were added to accompany and fill out the actions of the rite. Designed to deepen the spirituality of the priest, they often employed sacrificial terminology and at times were even understood as anticipating the meaning of the aucharistic prayer.

Thus the present missal helps clarify the nature of this rite, which is a prepration of the gifts (and the community) for the eucharistic prayer which will follow.

Bishops' Committee on the Liturgy
Newsletter, July-August, 1972.

**The preparation
of the gifts or
"offertory."**

64

65. Are the presider's formulas of praise ("Blessed be God . . .") at the preparation of the gifts to be said quietly or aloud?

Bishops' Committee on the Liturgy
Newsletter, July-August, 1972.

Again, the Bishops' Committee on the Liturgy clarifies this. If there is a procession with the gifts, the procession is accompanied by song or music. And this accompaniment should fill out the whole period till the priest is ready to say, "Pray, brethren . . ."

Thus it is not necessary that the priest's formula be heard by the people. In fact, the Order of Mass gives a variety of choices for the priest's prayers:

- the priest says the formula in a low voice during the singing; or
- if there is no singing or music, he says them quietly; or
- he may say them aloud; or
- if there is no song and if the priest says the formulas aloud, the people may say the acclamations at the end.

The Bishops' Committee goes on to say that "the decision to choose one or the other of the possibilities listed above may thus vary according to circumstances and the occasion . . ."

Avoid "ritual levelling."

It should be noted that the other formulas at this time, e.g., at the pouring of the wine and water, at the washing of hands, etc. are never to be said aloud. These are private, devotional formulas of the priest.

66. Why do we have a choice among eucharistic prayers?

In 1968 the National Conference of Catholic Bishops published a booklet which, first, affirmed the importance of the Roman Canon, and then explained why three alternatives to the canon were being introduced.

Four reasons for expanding the number of eucharistic prayers were given:

- concern about monotony in the repeated use of one prayer;
- worry about experimentation with unauthorized and poorly written eucharistic prayers;
- recognition that no one prayer can totally express the mystery of the eucharist;
- understanding of the defects as well as the merits of the Roman Canon.

Among such merits are: the Canon's ancient and traditional character, since it has been in use for some fifteen hundred years; the great flexibility provided by its variety of prefaces; its biblical language; and its theological precision, for example, in its theology of offering.

But there are a number of defects as well. For example, the publication points out that the intercessory prayers are split, some coming before and some after the institution narrative; note also the double list of saints. These references to offering are a glory of the prayer, but also a problem: "the repeated references to offering in the Roman Canon exaggerate it and obscure its relationship to the total picture." And it has long been obvious that the Roman Canon lacks an explicit reference to and theology of the Holy Spirit.

The New Eucharistic Prayers and Prefaces (Washington, DC: United States Catholic Conference, 1968).

Merits.

Defects.

Choice among eucharistic prayers.

66

85

67. What are the special characteristics of Eucharistic Prayers II, III, and IV?

The 1968 booklet from the National Conference of Catholic Bishops offered some brief reflections about each of the three new prayers.

Eucharistic Prayer II. Because of its brevity, concise language, and clear concepts, this text should be particularly effective for weekday Masses, home Masses, Masses for the young and small groups . . . This is substantially the text of Hippolytus—a eucharistic prayer which dates back to 215 A.D. There have been several modifications of the original version - the addition of the Sanctus and intercessions, an alteration in the doxology, and the clarification of more obscure phrases . . . The overall theme is Christ; the prayer addresses the Father in praise and thanksgiving for all that Jesus is and has done for us by forming a new people of God through his death and rising.

Eucharistic Prayer III. This prayer is especially suitable for Sundays and feasts; the text was deliberately designed to work well with both the old and new Roman prefaces. The key themes in this prayer are sacrifice and the Holy Spirit — with an obvious connection between the two. The opening section mentions the work of the Spirit in forming a worshipping community which will offer a clean sacrifice to God's glory. A familiar quotation ("from east to west . . .") from the prophet Malachi, often used by the Fathers in writing of the Eucharist, concludes that section.

A theology of sacrifice is developed in the memorial, offering, and communion invocation emphasizing the connection between the Holy Spirit and the sacrifice . . . We are one in the Spirit, one with Christ, one with ourselves, one with our neighbor. But it is 'this sacrifice, which has made our peace with you' that brings about the oneness and enables us to be at peace, love and union with God, ourselves, and the whole world.

Eucharistic Prayer IV. This prayer — longest of the three, yet shorter than the Roman Canon — is perhaps the most beautiful of the new texts. It contains real possibilities for teaching since its specific characteristic is a synthetic presentation of the total movement of salvation history. This panoramic summary is modeled upon the ancient tradition of the anaphoras or eucharistic prayers of Antioch, and it is developed in orderly fashion before the institutional narrative. Consequently the preface needs only to touch upon the themes of creation in general and the creation of the angels in particular. These first phrases in the history of salvation are further developed during a proclamation of the creation of man which follows the Sanctus. The compendium of the history of salvation is the reason why the preface must always be the same.

Every eucharistic prayer is essentially Trinitarian in structure. It is addressed to the Father, centers on the mystery of the Son, seeks extension into our lives and into the world around us through the power of the Holy Spirit. The fourth eucharistic prayer reflects this outline in its text. Uniquely, however, it gives a complete picture of human history and view of the Trinity within the prayer itself. Following the Sanctus, we speak of the Father creating man, of Christ saving him, of the Spirit who will 'complete his work on earth'.

The concept of the covenant looms as a central point, with additional notions of blood and sacrifice . . . The Eucharist is a sacrificial service, the blood of the Lord offered to God in sacrifice, acknowledging his absolute dominion over us and atoning for the sins of all mankind.

For full appreciation of the blood-covenant-sacrifice ideas we need the assistance of basic biblical scholarship. The fourth eucharistic prayer will of course teach and inspire by itself. But some further catechesis explaining these scriptural terms and their particular application to this eucharistic prayer will increase its value for people in the parish.

68. Will additional eucharistic prayers be approved?

Five already have been approved, provisionally, and have been available for us to use for years. They are all found in the sacramentary: two for Masses of Reconciliation, and three for Masses with Children.

Is it possible that we could have eucharistic prayers written and approved for the United States? This question was discussed at the June 1988 meeting of the Bishops' Committee on the Liturgy.

Bishops' Committee on the Liturgy *Newsletter*, June, 1988.

The question of additional eucharistic prayers for use in the United States was thoroughly discussed by the members, consultants, and advisors of the Liturgy Committee. The Committee was unanimous that more eucharistic prayers are needed. Many suggestions were made relative to the type and content of such prayers. It was agreed that a consultation book should be prepared which would present the eucharistic prayers approved for the United States as well as those approved for other countries.

68 **Additional eucharistic prayers.**

69. Why is the sign of peace included in the Mass?

The practice of extending a kiss of peace as a sign of respect or friendship is found in the Old Testament and is firmly rooted in Jewish tradition. We find witness to this practice in early Christian ritual, a borrowing from Jewish custom. For example, in the New Testament the kiss was a courteous preliminary to any ceremonial gathering, especially a meal. To omit it would cause remark or concern as when Christ said, "You gave me no kiss, but she has not ceased kissing my feet since I entered" (Lk 7:45). In the writings of St. Paul the kiss is recognized as a token of Christian communion (Rm 16:16; 1 Cor 16:20; 2 Cor 13:12). In 1 Peter 5:14 there is mention of an embrace: "Greet one another with the embrace of true love."

The kiss of peace in the liturgy is first mentioned at Rome by Justin Martyr (c. 150 A.D.) and is found in the Syrian Apostolic Constitutions (around the end of the fourth century). It was used in various prayer services as well as in the eucharistic celebration.

In the early Roman liturgical tradition the sign of peace, or the kiss of peace as it was called, followed the liturgy of the word. When the liturgy of the word became permanently joined to the liturgy of the eucharist, the general tendency was to associate the kiss of peace with the presentation of gifts. The admonition in Matthew about reconciling oneself with one's brother before bringing a gift to the altar encouraged this positioning of the kiss of peace in the Mass.

At a later stage, however, the kiss of peace was shifted to the conclusion of the eucharistic prayer, and finally, especially after St. Gregory the Great (d. 604), it became an appropriate extension of the Lord's Prayer in preparation for communion. The feeling was that since communion establishes and deepens the fellowship of Christ's body, the church, this gesture of peace and unity should be exchanged by all present before the actual participation in the body and blood of Christ.

A variety of positions.

The sign of peace. 69

89

70. What is the purpose of the Lamb of God chant? How long should it last?

Just as the gospel acclamation exists for the dual purposes of preparing the people to hear the gospel and of enhancing the processional movement to the pulpit, so also the Lamb of God chant exists to prepare us to receive holy communion and to provide an accompaniment to the ritual actions of breaking the eucharistic bread and pouring the precious blood.

A functional chant.

Thus the length of the chant is not limited to three acclamations, if the action takes longer, but neither should a musical setting go on long after the fraction is over.

Thus you can visualize what to do, for example, at a large concelebration, when it is going to take longer than usual to break, pour, and distribute to concelebrants. Instead of the usual three acclamations, followed by long and uncomfortable silence, the leader of song or choir should be prepared to use the first two acclamations as usual, and then to employ other scriptural titles and praises taken from the Mass of the day or elsewhere. Examples of tropes (expansions of sung parts of the Mass) would be: "Bread of Life, you feed your people with your own body and blood, have mercy on us"; "Prince of peace, you watch over your people with love, have mercy on us." New ones could be used, or old ones repeated, until the fraction and distribution to the priests are completed. Then the leader of song gives a prearranged signal to the congregation (raising a hand, for example) and the usual final acclamation ("Lamb of God, you take away the sins of the world, grant us peace") is sung.

71.

Why does our parish's missalette contain the statement "Guidelines for Receiving Communion"?

In 1986 the U.S. bishops voted to respond to what some believed to be an area of doubt in regard to who "may" or "may not" receive the eucharist. Significant numbers of non-Catholics and non-churchgoing Catholics have, usually at funerals, weddings, holidays, simply come forward to receive the eucharist.

Although not finding the complete answer to this question, the bishops decided that all participation aids and missalettes would henceforth contain a brief series of statements on this subject. The bishops had three goals in mind:

• to remind Catholics of the proper dispositions for receiving communion, including the use of the sacrament of penance when there is a consciousness of grave sin;

• to remind non-Catholics that we cannot offer them a general invitation to receive communion when they attend a Catholic marriage, funeral, or other eucharistic liturgy;

• to invite those who cannot receive communion to nevertheless be united in prayer with Catholics on these occasions.

These guidelines not only help create a climate of eucharistic respect, but also are an opportunity for explaining—with pastoral sensitivity—the church's discipline in this area.

See the Bishops' Committee on the Liturgy *Newsletter*, December, 1986.

72. Why do we keep hosts in the tabernacle?

One of the worries for clergy and sacristians who prepare the elements for eucharistic liturgy is that on occasion there may be a shortage of consecrated hosts. Even if this has happened only once, the remembered embarrassment and consequent anxiety in some cases have prompted an excessive response, namely, always to prepare many more hosts for communion than will be used at that Mass, and to keep the tabernacle filled with ciboria.

Many of us have seen the following: several ciboria filled to the top set out to be consecrated so that later on (a) there is small danger of running out, but (2) there will be continual withdrawals from the tabernacle.

An incorrect practice.

Certainly we do not wish to have a shortage of consecrated hosts, and yet continually withdrawing consecrated hosts from the tabernacle is theologically incorrect. As stated in the General Instruction of the Roman Missal: "It is most desirable that the faithful receive the Lord's body from hosts consecrated at the same Mass" (no. 56h).

Obviously, the principle that at each Mass every person should receive the Lord's body from hosts that were carried directly from the offertory table to the altar, rather than many people receiving the Lord's body from hosts that were brought from the tabernacle, needs to be grappled with. Assisting clergy too often go from the sacristy to the tabernacle, when in fact they should usually be going from the sacristy to the altar.

This point may seem trivial to some people because, in either case, it is the Lord whom they receive. But we ourselves are dull if we do not see the symbolic difference between receiving from the altar and receiving from the tabernacle. Remember that hosts are reserved in the tabernacle primarily for the sick and for adoration. Regularly, consciously, unabashedly using a tabernacle as a safeguard against not having enough hosts is an abuse of the explicit directive and value quoted above: "It is most desirable that the faithful receive the Lord's Body from hosts consecrated at the same Mass."

The goal.

Whereas there must always be some additional hosts in the tabernacle for those moments of surprise or error, our goal should be to consecrate just a little more than we need at any particular Mass. This means, for example, that if three hundred people usually communicate at the Saturday evening Mass, perhaps three hundred and thirty hosts—not one hundred or six hundred—should be brought up in the offertory procession.

72

Hosts in the tabernacle.

If possible, these hosts should all be in one vessel, just as the wine to be consecrated should be in one flagon. Then, while the Lamb of God is being sung, when assisting clergy or eucharistic ministers come to help, they come to the altar rather than to the tabernacle; and at the altar they pour the precious blood into the chalices carried to the altar at that time; and they apportion the eucharistic bread from one vessel on to the two or three plates or ciboria needed for the distribution.

The focus is to be on the altar, our eucharistic table, as it should be, and no one needs to go near the tabernacle until it is time to put away the remaining hosts. This powerfully shows the symbolism of the offertory procession and the eucharistic action: the ordinary gifts of bread and wine, presented by the community at that Mass, are placed on the altar in their midst, and from there these gifts are returned to them as the consecrated body and blood of our Savior.

The symbolism.

This theology might need a little preaching, and the practicalities might need a little practice; but after a while it will be second nature—it is what the church teaches and it makes sense. Adjustments and a different practice at certain Masses will be necessary. The hosts that are left over must be consumed at some Mass, perhaps the last Mass on Sunday, so that there are not too many in the tabernacle for the full week, and so that at every weekday Mass we can continue the same good principle of preparing, consecrating, and distributing the right amount for that particular community.

73.

We want to do an evaluation of our parish's Masses with children. Where do we start?

This Directory is printed toward the front of the sacramentary.

First, read the Directory for Masses with Children. Pay particular attention to which situation you are addressing. Is it a case of "Masses with Adults in which Children also Participate" (for example, First Communion Masses, Confirmation Masses, etc.)? Or is it a question of "Masses with Children in Which Only a Few Adults Participate" (for example, school Masses)?

Then you might want to ask some questions in collaboration with all who have a part in planning these celebrations. For example:

• Is there general satisfaction with the Masses of the previous year? Are the reasons liturgically valid? Pastorally sound?

• Did these Masses encourage Sunday participation?

• Have the permissions of the Directory been over-extended or under-used? Are the children tired of the ministerial roles, turned off to further participation before they become teenagers?

• Have these liturgies had a positive or negative effect on the children and adults who were present?

Such questions are not inconsequential. They center around the hard-to-decide issue of whether familiarity breeds contempt, and they poke around the subject of our own respect for the Transcendent.

73 **Evaluating Masses with children.**

74. Are there some other suggestions for the traditional school Mass on first Fridays?

To widen the spectrum of celebrations and to provide planners, preachers, and young people with more variety, a school might want to schedule a Mass each month using a more variable and liturgically sensitive pattern. For example:

September - Mass of the Holy Spirit
October - St. Francis of Assisi
November - A Mass for the Deceased
December - Mass of the Advent Season
January - Mass for Peace
February - Mass of the Lenten Season
March - St. Joseph
April - Mass of the Easter Season
May - Mass in Honor of Mary
June - Mass of the Sacred Heart

One reason to consider creating a new schedule and rationale for school Masses is that many years have passed since the first Friday practice began—years during which our liturgical life has drastically changed. With all good will, we simply may not have given enough thought to the obvious waning among the general population of first Friday devotion to the Sacred Heart, and to the liturgical priorities that we could now be teaching. If first Friday Masses have become an empty tradition, meaning that few teachers or students really know why this day was chosen, or can compellingly assert that it should be maintained, then either new vitality must be imparted—or new wineskins be pressed into use.

Now more than ever, when Sunday Mass attendance is diminished, it seems clear that we have a greater responsibility to provide prayerful liturgies for the young people in our care, under our influence, during the week. It is a new ball game; we have to win allegiance to eucharistic worship one child at a time. Every poorly planned and poorly celebrated Mass hurts our cause. Every good one helps it.

75. What freedom do I have in selecting readings for Masses with children?

Don't bore.

There is a large degree of flexibility available to us when celebrating Mass with children and youth.

For example, when the children are coming to Mass on a weekday of ordinary time, check the readings before anyone selects music or begins to prepare the reader. See if the readings make sense to you. Try to imagine yourself preaching about them. If even one does not make sense to you, then the liturgy of the word will most likely bore the children and diminish their respect for and expectations about the word.

In such a situation the readings can be changed. We don't want pick and choose only the parts of Scripture that appeal to us, but neither are we (and the children) doomed to exercises in futility. The Directory for Masses with Children is quite clear: "If all the readings assigned to the day seem to be unsuited to the capacity of the children, it is permissible to choose readings or a reading either from the Lectionary for Mass or directly from the Bible, taking into account the liturgical season" (no. 43).

Respect the children and the readings.

What is being encouraged is "care." The continuous readings are fine for most of us daily churchgoers, but on the one day a month a class or a school comes to Mass, make sure they have solid food that will feed them. Pick a good clear story or a practical section from an epistle rather than a wandering historical saga or a prophecy the children cannot situate. If the gospel passage is too brief or disconnected, select a longer section, giving the suitable introduction and conclusion, so that it makes sense to them. And if even the best young reader(s) are weak, replace them with strong impressive adults. We must be committed to the readings. We must make certain that they are respectably proclaimed. Otherwise, we will betray the word by ignoring it.

75

Selecting readings.

76. What do you think about children serving as readers at First Communion Masses?

Several years ago I attended a study day devoted to the topic "The Child at Worship." One of the catechists present remarked: "You blow a child's whole ecclesiology right out of the water by having him or her be a lector at a First Holy Communion Mass, when every Sunday an adult is the one to proclaim the readings. If you asked any group of children who should read at their First Holy Communion Mass, the answer would most probably be: the teacher or the person in charge of the program. Children want order and quality in their lives too."

This points to the key topic of quality. All of us have seen outstanding service by youngsters in various roles, especially youthful readers who outshine adults. Yet, out of kindness or hope, we have not deflected less talented children from going to the pulpit, and thus allowed times when no one knew what the word was about. At other times, all attention was on the reader rather than the message. Even if we did not recall the exact principle—that the reader should be so good as to be unnoticed—we felt uneasy. As when a barely controlled mourner tries to be a lector, we realize the difficulty of paying attention to the word, and we sense the inappropriateness of that person reading at that time.

Quality is the key.

Does this mean that children should never read at Mass? By no means. I just want to raise the possibility that we may have allowed the pendulum to swing too far, and that a readjustment may now be appropriate. The place to start is the Directory for Masses with Children, especially its classification as to whether children are part of, or are the whole, congregation.

Just asking the question.

Children as readers.

76

77. Is it advisable to allow children to receive from the cup at their First Communion Masses?

There is no specific place to look for direction on this in the official liturgical books besides the General Instruction on the Roman Missal (nos. 240-242), where we are reminded that holy communion has a more complete form as a sign when it is received under both kinds, and that the faithful should be guided towards a desire to receive under both kinds.

Building on that, the liturgical commission of my own archdiocese several years ago formulated this advice.

Offer the cup.

1. . . . .generally speaking, the cup should be offered to children at first communion:

a. because the church tells us communion under this form is a more complete sign of the eucharistic banquet, and because the Instruction urges that the faithful be guided towards a desire for reception of the eucharist under both forms. While all parishes are not yet capable of offering communion from the cup, it is the view of the Commission that parishes should be moving toward that goal;

b. because the purpose of preparation for communion is to prepare the child for his or her future experience with the eucharist, it is important that the child be prepared for communion under the form of wine at the time of preparation for first communion. It is not unusual for individuals to attend Mass in places other than their own parish, and it is likely that the child will have the experience of being offered communion from the cup, even if this is not regularly done in his or her own parish. If this preparation is not given at the time of first communion, it is not likely to be given at all.

But consult.

2. The decision about whether to offer communion from the cup to children at first communion should be made by the pastor in consultation with his staff and parish council.

And consider.

3. From a pastoral and educational point of view, the following elements should be seriously considered:

• if communion is offered under both forms, the child should be permitted to make the decision about whether or not to receive from the cup, just as he or she decides whether to receive in the hand or on the tongue.

• Part of the preparation for first communion should include a taste of wine, just as children are given unconsecrated

77 **Children receiving from the cup.**

hosts as part of their preparation. This should not be done without the permission of parents.

+ The matter of alcoholism should be considered and parents should be alerted that if there is alcoholism in the family the parents should be actively involved in the child's decision whether or not to receive from the cup.

+ In a similar way, where there is a parental concern for hygiene, this should be respected.

4. Catechists responsible for preparing children for first communion should be familiar with the General Instruction of the Roman Missal and with *This Holy and Living Sacrifice: Directory for the Celebration and Reception of Communion under Both Kinds*, published by the United States Catholic Conference.

Do some reading.

78. In our parish tensions sometimes arise between sacramental preparation coordinators and parish clergy. How can we avoid this?

Reasons for discontent.

It seems that winter and spring can indeed be seasons of discontent for religious educators and clergy. As first sacramental moments arise, there is the possibility of disappointment and even anger if there has not been discussion and agreement beforehand. The good people who work all year preparing children for penance, eucharist, and confirmation can feel very hurt if clergy change their plans or requirements at the last moment; and the good people who have ultimate responsibility for the children's preparation may feel let down by the coordinator if something unexpected is to be done or if the children seem ignorant of basics. The failure to communicate during the summer and fall, and/or to stick to what was mutually decided, is very upsetting to everyone and works against the best interests of children and their families. More than outsiders know, discord can cast a pall over important days for both coordinators and clergy, and is a direct cause of poorly planned and celebrated ceremonies.

A suggestion.

Even with the best of intentions, misunderstandings can occur. A practical suggestion is that if a crisis arises as a celebration is about to begin, we priests should go along with the plan of the coordinators. More often than not, we share the blame for not planning ahead, or for failing to voice objections and propose improvements when first told of something. Even if we are uncomfortable on that occasion, it is more respectful of the other person's expertise to follow his/her plan, is more considerate of the children's expectations, and is a stronger inducement to be actively involved in the planning next time.

78 Avoiding tensions.

79. What are some good texts for preaching at First Communion Masses?

Many priests know from experience that we can be victims of our own overactivity or carelessness, and arrive at First Communion day with no particular gospel or homily in mind. It is ironic: those proclaiming the first readings have the texts prepared, and the preacher has not yet picked a gospel. And to compound the problem, many preachers are not enthusiastic about the choices they see in the lectionary when they open it to no. 909 (Holy Eucharist) and realize that the selections are rather long and abstract for a First Communion congregation of excited and nervous people.

Whether the children read or not (and there are differences of opinion about the wisdom of actively involving the children, with some saying that taking this role is too nerve-wracking and distracting, while others see greater benefits than drawbacks in having many of the children perform some service), it does seem essential that the readings at a First Communion Mass be simple, short, and stimulating, and that the homily be described in these words as well.

Simple, short, and stimulating readings.

Especially since we want to preach a homily rather than a generalized sermon, early attention to all the scripture choices pays off. Before the first reader prepares, the homilist and other planners should all like the readings. There is no point in choosing the unusual story of Elijah under the broom tree and rehearsing it to perfection if the homilist hates it and would never even refer to it.

In planning a Mass for First Communion, there is no rule about whether to have two readings or three, but I suggest the principle that we should help the children see the similarity between this special Mass and the Sunday Masses celebrated each week. If you do choose to have three readings, you might like two very clear passages—Acts 2:42-47, about the apostles sharing everything in common, and 1 Corinthians 11:23-26, about the Last Supper—followed by a eucharistic gospel not included in the no. 909 selection, for example, Luke 14:15-24, about the man who gave a great feast and had his guests fail to show up for a variety of poor reasons.

Two readings or three?

Another homiletic possibility which is always open to us is to preach about the Mass itself or some element within it. Many people would benefit from some restatement of the importance, origin, effectiveness, uniqueness, and/or history of the Mass, especially as it applies to that moment when their children begin to sacramentally share such a glorious and life-giving tradition.

Texts for preaching. **79**

80. What are the advantages of the Rite of Christian Initiation of Adults?

The many parishes that have begun to employ the Rite of Christian Initiation of Adults (RCIA) testify that this ritual offers our best blueprint for inviting, evangelizing, and celebrating the initiation of non-baptized adults into our community. The RCIA process, in contrast to the rather private convert classes run by clergy in past years, aims at involving the whole parish community in knowing, praying for, and supporting new members. The priests are involved, but so are other members of the parish: deacons, catechists, godparents, sponsors, friends. There is to be a team effort on behalf of the candidates. We have heard busy people express the fear that the RCIA is too much work for too few people. This fear is unfounded, and the work is rewarding for some of the following reasons.

A public process.

A rewarding process.

• The RCIA has an impact on the whole parish, impressing those who are already initiated. It causes cradle Catholics to take a new look at themselves and the importance of their own baptism: "If another adult goes through all this for what I already have . . . then maybe what I already have is worth a higher appraisal and a deeper commitment."

• The RCIA makes conversion a public affair, known to the whole parish. The preparation of the candidates includes being at church and being introduced and being prayed for. Candidates who have hesitated at first and then given this public process a chance have declared that they liked it. In emotional terms, it certainly surpasses a private baptism. In ecclesiological terms, it definitely shows that initiation is into a *community*.

• The RCIA reminds the whole parish—through bulletin announcements, invitations, liturgical ceremonies, and especially the Easter Vigil—that we are all supposed to be fishers, feeders, and friends in Christ. If there are barriers or prejudices among us, listening to prospective members is a good way to notice the problems in our parish and start to repair them. A welcoming community will be a reconciling community.

• The RCIA focuses on the basics of belief—the life, death, and resurrection of Jesus Christ. This is crucial to all evangelization, including the ongoing teaching of the already initiated.

• The RCIA asks us to be patient. It does not produce "90 day wonders." To some degree, it plans on making it hard to become a Catholic—so that when a person makes a commitment, a person stays committed.

80

The RCIA.

81. What does the RCIA look like in practice?

To summarize in a few words, let us say that a typical catechumenate program begins with a commitment from people in the parish—any combination of clergy, religious, and/or lay—to study and implement the RCIA. Although the RCIA is flexible and open-ended, many parishes follow the rhythms of the school year, beginning in the fall and ending with the post-baptismal catechesis after Easter. Spring and summer bulletin announcements and personal invitation to non-Catholics who are known at the church would be another step. By September/October, if any people have expressed an interest, group meetings could begin. If no one comes forward, which is a disappointment that happens periodically, then you simply wait till next year. (But you know in advance that you will be a little let-down at the Easter Vigil; not having adults to initiate is like not having a favorite team in the World Series.)

Flexible.

Technically, this first period of inquiry in the fall is called the **pre-catechumenate**. There is no commitment at this stage, only the satisfying of curiosity and the sifting of interests. This period ends with the coming of Advent, when those who wish enter the order of catechumens.

Yet four periods.

The second timeframe, that of the **catechumenate**, can last for years, but most often this period of evangelization leads the people to make a definite commitment on an early Sunday of Lent. The catechumens are then "elected" for initiation, and the third stage of their journey—**election** or **enrollment of names**—coincides with the season of Lent. This is a special time for them for purification and enlightenment, for the scrutinies and the presentations, in preparation for baptism, confirmation, and eucharist at the all-important Easter Vigil.

The final period is a time for **mystagogy** or post-baptismal catechesis. During the Easter season the neophytes continue to meet and get deeper into the mystery of faith and enjoy the sacramental life of the church.

The RCIA in practice.

81

82. Is there a place in the RCIA for those who have already been baptized?

The RCIA is for the unbaptized.

The RCIA, we must remember, is primarily for those who have never, in any church, at any time, been baptized with water in the name of the Father, Son, and Holy Spirit.

Nevertheless, parishes often have three groups of adult people who need spiritual care and feeding: the unbaptized who want to join the church; those who have already been baptized in other churches and want to become Catholics; and baptized Catholics who never had religious instructions or other sacraments, and who now want to make up what they missed. We must provide for all three groups, without treating them identically. This would be wrong. The RCIA has much to teach us about general religious values, but only the unbaptized can be catechumens and go through all the stages of the RCIA.

Candidates for full communion.

Those who have already been baptized, for example, in the Episcopal or Lutheran or Baptist Church, and who now wish to become members of the Catholic Church are called "candidates" as they prepare for full communion with the Catholic Church. Some of the points to be remembered are the following.

- The sacrament of baptism may not be repeated.
- Any treatment of the candidates as though they were catechumens is to be absolutely avoided.
- Baptized Christians are to receive both doctrinal and spiritual preparation, according to their needs. As they grow in their spiritual adherence to the Catholic Church, we hope they will find the fullness of their baptism.
- It is the responsibility of the bishop to receive baptized Christians into full communion. But the priest to whom he entrusts the celebration of the rite of admission can administer the sacrament of confirmation during that rite.
- The rite should be seen as a celebration of the bond between the candidate and the parish community; its climax is the reception of holy communion.
- If the reception into the church takes place within Mass (as it ordinarily will, at the Easter Vigil), the candidates, according to their consciences, should confess their sins beforehand.
- At their reception candidates should be accompanied by one or two sponsors. Afterwards, the names of those who have been received into full communion with the Catholic Church should be entered in a special book, noting the date and place of their baptism, and the date and place of their reception into the Catholic Church.

82 **Those who have already been baptized.**

83. Is it permissible for candidates for Confirmation to wear stoles at the ceremony?

The problem with candidates wearing stoles is one of mixing metaphors. The candidates, who are in fact celebrating a sacrament of initiation, are wearing stoles, which are really the liturgical clothing of the ordained. While these stoles are often tastefully decorated with religious symbols and with the person's confirmation name, and while decorating them helps the candidates to be more involved in the preparation for their sacrament, there is a fundamental dissonance about this practice.

A number of years ago the Bishops' Committee on the Liturgy addressed this question.

Bishops' Committee on the Liturgy *Newsletter*, December, 1984.

> The traditional vesture of the newly baptized is the white robe. There is no indication in liturgical tradition that the stole—which properly is the vesture of ordained ministers—was used for neophytes.
>
> The current practice in some places of using stoles at confirmation seems to have arisen out of the laudable desire to provide a symbol signifying the confirmands' participation in the life and ministry of the Church. However, the distinction between the universal priesthood of all the baptized and the ministerial priesthood of the ordained is blurred when the distinctive garb of ordained ministers is used in this manner.
>
> To emphasize the relationship between confirmation and baptism, a white garment might be used at confirmation—just as the baptismal robe was used to clothe the newly baptized. Use of a stole, however, should be avoided for the reason already indicated.

Stoles at confirmation.

83

84. May parents be sponsors of their own children at Confirmation?

The rite itself.

The short answer is "no." The long answer also gets to "no" but takes a few twists and turns. To get our liturgical bearings here, let us start with no. 5 of the Rite of Confirmation:

> Ordinarily there should be a sponsor for each of those to be confirmed. The sponsor brings the candidate to receive the sacrament, presents him to the minister for the anointing, and will later help him to fulfill his baptismal promises faithfully under the influence of the Holy Spirit.

> In view of contemporary pastoral circumstances, it is desirable that the godparent at baptism, if available, also be the sponsor at confirmation. This change expresses more clearly the relationship between baptism and confirmation and also makes the function and responsibility of the sponsor more effective.

> Nonetheless the option of a special sponsor for confirmation is not excluded. Even the parents themselves may present their children for confirmation. It is for the local Ordinary the determine diocesan practice in the light of local circumstances.

This part of the Introduction to the Rite of Confirmation has seen slight modifications over the past years, yet the key statement about parents being allowed to present their children for confirmation (coming right after mention of "special sponsors") has not been deleted from the text, even after the appearance of the new Code of Canon Law.

A clarification.

So in practice, are parents to be sponsors at confirmation? An official clarification was given by the Congregation for the Sacraments and Divine Worship.

> 1. As far as possible, a candidate for confirmation should have a sponsor.
> 2. According to the directives in canon 893 (with reference to canon 874, 5) neither the father nor the mother of a candidate can be a sponsor.
> 3. However, even when there is a sponsor, parents may present their child for confirmation. By "present" is meant the simple fact of bringing or accompanying the candidate to the bishop.

84

Parents as sponsors of their own children.

106

There would seem to be no contradiction between canon 893 (cf. also canon 874, 5) and the Rite of Confirmation, nos. 5 and 21. Parents and sponsors have different functions. Parents can present their children in the way intended by the rite, even though they cannot be sponsors.

The *Newsletter* article concludes: "In light of this clarification, it should be emphasized that, in those cases when no godparent is present, a parent presenting a child for confirmation should not be called a godparent or sponsor, nor be understood as assuming the role of godparent. Perhaps the best designation for the parent would be 'presenter'."

This clarification is found in the Bishops' Committee on the Liturgy *Newsletter*, December, 1983.

85. What are the advantages of communal penance services?

Let us say, first of all, that a communal penance service is usually composed of prayer, scripture readings, preaching, examination of conscience, and act of contrition prayed in common. All this prepares people for individual confession and individual absolution, if the people wish to receive these. Very appropriately, it has both public and private elements. For example, the Introduction to the Rite of Penance (no. 5) says:

> By the hidden and loving mystery of God's design, men are joined together in the bonds of supernatural solidarity, so much so that the sin of one harms the others, just as the holiness of one benefits the others. Penance always entails reconciliation with our brothers and sisters who are always harmed by our sins.

Drawing people together.

The "supernatural solidarity" that the rite speaks of needs to be fleshed out for forgetful people by drawing congregations together to contemplate the reality and viciousness of sin. Long years of training have made many of us individualists, people who think basically only of private sins and private absolutions. Communal services do not advocate or employ general absolution; they do give a person the chance to speak personally with a confessor. Thus they do broaden the experience of life and can—especially for those who have stopped going to confession—provide a re-entry point, as this sacrament is *celebrated* in a more familiar and less isolated way than happens week after week in what are nearly empty churches.

People supporting people.

Try for a moment to see the way this sacrament is administered through the eyes of a repentant sinner who seeks forgiveness. Whereas some people do appreciate the anonymity and solitary atmosphere of regular confession times, I think that the liturgical reforms have made going to confession in dark churches when very few people are around a strange experience. Even parishes that hear many confessions benefit from the hustle and bustle, as people feel their sorrow for sin and their need for confession *legitimated* by the many others who congregate for the same purpose. I believe in the great value of penance services, that they can help people come back to the church and to the sacrament, in part because reconciliation is *celebrated* at a service and people do not feel so alone because at least some other people are there to ask for forgiveness, too.

85 Communal penance services.

When we add the fact that religious education programs aim at joyful, reverent celebrations for the first time a child receives the sacrament of penance, and that parents are urged to accompany the child to these services, we are dealing with a new tradition that has been well received.

Other advantages of communal penance services are:

- the role of God's word is emphasized;
- preaching can help people realize the variety of sins and their implications and consequences;
- young and old acknowledge weakness and sorrow and make promises to reform in one another's hearing;
- we see one another in a new and more sympathetic light;
- we find it easier to admit our faults when others admit theirs;
- we can exchange signs of peace within the ceremony, and we can hear loving words of forgiveness from one another as well as from the priest;
- we can make this sacrament more of a family and community affair.

86. Must a communal penance service include the sacrament of reconciliation?

A communal penance service ordinarily does include the sacrament of reconciliation, but does not have to do so. In fact, it should be made clear that coming to such a service does not require a person to go to confession. People can come, pray, and leave without receiving the sacrament at that time.

A penance service can be an excellent way to prepare for individual confession and absolution, either at that time or later on. But there is also the option of having a non-sacramental penitential service, with or without a priest, for the times when we simply need to be reminded of our sinfulness and God's mercy, or when we are not ready or able to receive sacramental absolution, as, for example, in the case of children before their first confession, or adults in invalid marriages.

86 **Penance services and reconciliation.**

87.

What are some factors to consider in our efforts to encourage people to celebrate the sacrament of penance during Lent?

There are, I believe, four particularly important factors here: realism, repetition, respect, and re-education.

Realism. Whether this question is discussed by clergy, parish staff, or the liturgy committee, an accurate sense of who goes to confession when, and who is not going and why, is the first thing to be considered. No parish gets all its people to this sacrament each Lent. All one can do is increase the percentage, and prepare the ground for other seasons. And in the interests of integrity, make it clear that this is, legally speaking, an optional sacrament; according to canon law, the only people bound to approach this sacrament are those who have committed grave sin. It might be a rewarding experience to make the case for coming to confession, as recommended in canon 988, even for venial sins. I think that is the battleground for credibility for this sacrament: to grant that most of our hearers are not awful sinners, but that they are hurting inside, and then convince them that this sacrament can help to heal them.

Many people hurt inside.

Repetition. People are bombarded with advertising for weeks before they are expected to buy a new product. So too we cannot expect that one warm invitation, or the weekly listing of the times for confession, will be sufficient to break down years of hesitation. People need to be invited and notified over and over again. Something special must be done to dramatize the fact that *now* is the time to celebrate reconciliation. And this is helpful not only for the wandering sheep; for those who already are willing, we could do more to promote the equation that "Lent = Reconciliation."

People need to be invited.

Respect. Anyone who has been casually or negligently treated by a doctor, counselor, or confidant, should have a sense of how vulnerable a penitent is in the hands of a confessor. Many people have stopped going to confession because of a real or imagined disagreement or criticism that was perceived as a personal attack, as a lack of respect. The medical dictum "Do no harm" should help us priests be extra careful when we feel ourselves getting impatient, angry, ready to cut a person off. Especially when the penitent is anonymous and invisible to us, we can make mistakes in judgment, in tone of voice, in attempts at humor, that can wound a person's heart and soul. People want to be respected, to be understood. This is part of the healing of the sacrament.

Penitents are vulnerable.

Re-education. The work of making people familiar and comfortable with all the new rituals is far from over. In fact, we are not doing enough ongoing education about the Mass and the sacraments. Half the population in front of us today wasn't even going to

The sacrament of penance during Lent.

87

Continue to educate.

church at the time the post-Vatican II changes were first introduced, and it is incorrect to believe that all who were in church got the whole message in perfect order. For something like penance, which carries an aura of mystery, a burden of memories, and a worrisome complexity for the unpracticed, there ought to be annual or semi-annual refreshers in the form of homilies and literature. For example, acting out a confession, as a demonstration and teaching tool within the homily time, can spark a tremendous renewal of interest. Another thing that might be done every Lent is to hand out with a parish bulletin a guide or outline for people to look over and even bring with them to confession.

88. Who should receive the anointing of the sick?

If people are periodically reminded that there is a meaning in suffering, and if the sick and the healthy are brought together in prayer, then some of the dread that people have about sickness and old age can be dispelled. Instead of denying illness or infirmities, example and encouragement should be given to those who are eligible for the anointing of the sick. The General Introduction answers the question about who should be anointed, and this should be repeatedly presented to the people so that they will know to ask for this sacrament.

> The Letter of James states that the sick are to be anointed in order to raise them up and save them. Great care and concern should be taken to see that those of the faithful whose health is seriously impaired by sickness or old age should receive this sacrament.

Pastoral Care of the Sick: Rites of Anointing and Viaticum, no. 8.

This quotation has a footnote explaining the use of the word "seriously."

An important footnote.

> The word *periculose* has been carefully studied and rendered as "seriously," rather than "gravely," "dangerously," or "perilously." Such a rendering will serve to avoid restrictions upon the celebration of the sacrament. On the one hand, the sacrament may and should be given to anyone whose health is seriously impaired; on the other hand, it may not be given indiscriminately or to any person whose health is not seriously impaired.

As you read these other directives from the General Introduction, please be aware that even your 1983 edition has language that has been changed to conform with the new Code of Canon Law.

Further considerations.

• The sacrament may be repeated if the person's condition becomes more serious, or if the person recovers and then again falls ill.
• A sick person may be anointed before surgery whenever a serious illness is the reason for the surgery.
• Elderly persons may be anointed if they have become noticeably weakened even though no serious illness is present.
• Sick children should be anointed if they have sufficient use of reason to be strengthened by this sacrament.

Determining those to be anointed.

• Mentally ill people, who are judged to have a serious mental illness and who would be strengthened by the sacrament, may be anointed.

• Finally, in those happy cases where someone does benefit physically from the anointing, no. 40c of the Rite makes an excellent suggestion which coincides with human reactions and should be mentioned, viz., "Sick persons who regain their health after being anointed should be encouraged to give thanks for the favor received by participating in a Mass of thanksgiving or by some other suitable means."

Sacraments are for the living.

Part of reality is that the priest is sometimes not called until a sick person has died, and there are other times when a previously healthy person suddenly expired. Since all sacraments are for the living, when a priest is called to attend someone who has already died, he should not administer the sacrament, but instead pray to God to forgive the person's sins and receive him or her into the kingdom.

89.
Our parish liturgy committee would like to begin a parish catechesis on the Order of Christian Funerals. Any ideas on how to go about this?

Why not begin with the introduction to the rite? Nos. 1-49 set the theological and pastoral context for this ministry. There are also other important paragraphs but they are not so easy to find. The following is a list of such sections within the ritual, with my own identification or summary.

52. What the church tries to do when a member dies.
56. The purpose of a vigil (which we call a "wake").
64. Why members of the parish should come to the vigil.
101. Prayers to say right after death.
109. Prayers for the first visit to the funeral home.
119. Prayers at the end of the vigil.
131. The significance of receiving the body at the church.
133. Description of the rite of reception.
137. Why we read the word of God at funerals.
141. What a funeral homily should do for the community.
143. Sharing the eucharist is a foretaste of eternal life.
146. Why we have a final commendation.
150. Why we seek full, active participation of the community.
154. Why the church encourages the celebration of Mass.
206. The rite of committal as a sign of hope and unity.

Your committee could, for example, run a series in the parish bulletin. Just quote the appropriate sections from the rite or, if you want to be creative, also give a short introduction to each statement. We need to remind people of the church's practices at the time of death and what these practices mean.

Order of Christian Funerals (Washington, DC: United States Catholic Conference, 1985).

Again, continue to educate.

Catechesis on the Order of Funerals

89

90. Is there anything we should keep in mind as to people with disabilities receiving the sacraments?

Bishop Sullivan's article appeared in *America*, April 19, 1986.

Bishop Walter Sullivan of Richmond, Virginia, has written that the Code of Canon Law definitely includes retarded and otherwise disabled persons among those eligible for the sacraments and for sacramental preparation programs. He makes the following basic points.

• Handicapped persons are part of the Christian faithful, not a segregated segment; they have rights and duties, including participation in the sacraments.

• Sacraments are not a reward for the perfect but a grace for all pilgrims. They should not be seen as isolated moments, but as special experiences within an ongoing, total church experience.

• The "age of discretion" basically means being able to feel differently toward good and evil, and being able to desire the good. Since even a severely disabled person can experience a longing for the good, "age of discretion" is not an absolute norm and must not be used to bar people from sacraments.

• The new Code of Canon Law encourages that a mentally retarded adult be evangelized and catechized as fully as possible before baptism. This could mean a catechumenate program geared to this person's level. The person should surely participate in activities with other catechumens and the worshiping community.

• All baptized people are obliged by canon 890 to be confirmed. This obligation certainly includes the handicapped, and the implications of canons 889-891 do permit mentally retarded people to participate in confirmation.

• After proper preparation, any child (or adult) who can distinguish between ordinary food and the body of Christ should be permitted to receive the eucharist. As Bishop Sullivan says, "Retarded children are very capable of receiving Communion reverently, especially by imitating those around them."

• Penance should be an option for the individual, because one individual might be capable of receiving Communion but incapable of sin. However, another person with a disability might be very capable of receiving the eucharist and of sinning and repenting.

• Two key points are to be kept in mind concerning the anointing of the sick: a) if there is any chance that a person understands the meaning of his or her sickness, the sacrament of anointing can be conferred; b) there is no justification for the indiscriminate anointing of all persons with disabilities. A disability is a permanent

90

People with disabilities and the sacraments.

physical condition rather than a sickness. Handicapped people should only be anointed in times of serious sickness or old age.

• The new Code drops the old impediments to Holy Orders that arose from physical deformities, disabilities, and epilepsy. It adds a new one: psychic defect, that is, something that makes a candidate incapable of rightly carrying out the ministry.

• The primary focus regarding marriage is whether those two people can enter a covenant relationship and build a partnership for life.

91. Can you suggest any form of liturgical prayer that more Catholics should know about?

A spiritual adventure.

There is one such form that I can especially recommend. It is the official prayer of the church, the prayer that shapes and sanctifies each day. It is called the Liturgy of the Hours. While it is a special responsibility of clergy and religious, it is a treasure that is open to all.

To adapt the Navy recruiting message, being a Christian is more than a job—it is an adventure. Adventures are not always pleasant. There can be side trips into disappointments and conflicts. We all need spiritual refreshment. We all need to concentrate on our prayer life. And the Liturgy of the Hours is the perfect medium for this.

Everyone should read and reread the General Instruction of the Liturgy of the Hours. This document is always printed in the books themselves. It will really help you. Sure, you can jump in and start to drive your car without ever checking the instruction manual—but you might drive your car into an accident or into the ground. Subsequent frustration might even lead you to decide to do without a car. At the very least you will not get all the benefits and satisfaction that the designers intended.

Read the General Instruction.

The General Instruction is printed in front of the first volume of the four volume set of the Liturgy of the Hours. Reading it is a reminder and encouragement to imitate Christ and constantly persevere in prayer. There are lots of statements worth pondering:

- public common prayer by the people of God is rightly considered to be among the primary duties of the Church (no. 1);
- the purpose of the Liturgy of the Hours includes the sanctification of the day and of the whole range of human activity (no. 11);
- the Liturgy of the Hours is an excellent preparation for the Eucharist, because it inspires and deepens the dispositions we need for a fruitful celebration of the Eucharist: faith, hope, love, devotion, and a spirit of self-denial (no. 12);
- the Liturgy of the Hours, like other liturgical actions, is not something private, but belongs to the whole community . . . Where possible, the principal hours should be celebrated communally in church . . . Those in holy orders have the responsibility of initiating and directing the prayer of the community (no. 20, 21, 22);

91

Liturgy of the Hours.

• the Liturgy of the Hours is entrusted to sacred ministers in such a special way that even when the faithful are not present it should be recited by individuals . . . The bishop should be the first of all the members of his Church in offering prayer . . . Priests, united as they are with the bishop and the whole presbyterium, are themselves representative in a special way of Christ the priest, and so share the same responsibility of praying to God for the people entrusted to them, and indeed for the whole world (no. 28).

These quotes come just from the early part of the document, the chapter emphasizing the importance of the Liturgy of the Hours in the life of the Church and individuals within it. An annual reading of this material could only help to reinvigorate and reaffirm our commitment to do this prayer, and to lead others to join us.

Inexpensive one volume editions of the Liturgy of the Hours are available. With encouragement and instruction individuals would gladly buy their own copies, and others could be purchased and kept on hand for general use. They are the kind of books that could become the ordinary opening prayerbooks of most parish societies and councils.

92. Do the stations of the cross have any relevance today? Where did this devotion come from?

It is true that the stations of the cross have lost some of their popularity in recent decades. One reason for this is, of course, that the primary expressions of our worship life have been reformed and accepted. Nevertheless, the stations are a very powerful expression of faith in the humanity of Jesus; they are a form of participating in the sufferings of his cross.

Some history.

This devotion has its roots and first elaboration in fourth-century Jerusalem. Up to that time the death-and-resurrection of the Lord Jesus was celebrated in a unified, single-night observance. But under the influence of St. Cyril—who was in charge of the catechumens and later became bishop of Jerusalem—a more developed, week-long observance of the "Holy Week" events became popular.

What Cyril originally did for the catechumens— gathering them for a Palm Sunday procession from the Mount of Olives into the city, telling them where to meet him at certain hours on Wednesday, Thursday, Friday, Saturday, filling their whole week with on-site prayers and commemoration—was embraced by many who were already initiated. Cyril's genius was to help fourth-century believers commemorate first-century events and to do so with the benefit of being at special places at special times of the year. Another stage in the history of the stations revolves around the Franciscans who were placed in charge of the sacred places in the Holy Land. In the fifteenth century the custom began of erecting a series of little shrines to commemorate the various events associated with the passion and death of Jesus. At first there was a lot of freedom; whoever designed a particular shrine could choose the number of stations and their themes. Not till the decision of Pope Clement XII in 1731 was there agreement on having fourteen stations. Soon afterwards, devotion to the stations spread rapidly throughout Europe, largely through the preaching of St. Leonard of Port Maurice, a Franciscan priest.

Value for today.

There are at least three themes that this devotion helps us reinforce: God's love and mercy for us sinful people; the terrible physical suffering and mental anguish that Our Lord endured; a deep sorrow for our sins. It would be a loss if we did not try to use and improve this unique devotional aspect of our religious heritage.

92

Stations of the cross.

93. Where can I learn more about Benediction of the Blessed Sacrament?

One source is *Eucharistic Worship and Devotion outside Mass*. Also known as "Study Text 11," this is part of a series of excellent and practical booklets on liturgical topics created over the last fifteen years by the Secretariat of the Bishops' Committee on the Liturgy.

These texts have a documentary role to play in educating people about liturgical principles and consequent actions. Each Study Text quotes from many official sources. For example, regarding Benediction, people should know that in his apostolic letter of February 1980, "On the Mystery and Worship of the Holy Eucharist," Pope John Paul II encouraged personal prayer before the Blessed Sacrament, hours of adoration, periods of exposition (short, prolonged, and annual), eucharistic benediction, eucharistic processions, and eucharistic congresses.

Other official sources include the 1973 Roman document "Holy Communion and Worship of the Eucharist outside Mass." Reprinting sections like these in a parish's weekly bulletin can help people better understand the history of our eucharistic developments.

These documents may be ordered from USCC Publishing Services, 3241 Fourth St., NE, Washington, DC 20017.

The primary and original reason for reservation of the eucharist outside Mass is the administration of viaticum. The secondary ends are the giving of communion and the adoration of our Lord Jesus Christ present in the sacrament. The reservation of the sacrament for the sick led to the praiseworthy practice of adoring this heavenly food that is reserved in churches. This cult of adoration has a sound and firm foundation, especially since faith in the real presence of the Lord has as its natural consequence the outward, public manifestation of that belief (no. 5).

In the celebration of Mass, the chief ways in which Christ is present in his Church emerge clearly one after the other. First he is present in the very assembly of the faithful gathered together in his name; next, he is present in his word, with the reading and explanation of Scripture in the church; also in the person of the minister; finally, and above all, in the eucharistic elements (no. 6).

Benediction.

93

No. 8 states that pastors should see to it that for several hours each day the faithful should be able to pray in the presence of the blessed sacrament.

The place for the reservation of the eucharist should be truly preeminent. It is highly recommended that the place be suitable also for private adoration and prayer . . . This will be achieved more easily if the chapel is separate from the body of the church . . . (no. 9).

94. Why should we have prayer services with people of other faiths?

Ecumenical and interfaith services should be essential and integral to each parish's participation in its community. Dialogues, discussion groups, joint political action—these are all acceptable forms of actualizing the unity of hearts and souls that we should desire. But none of these measure up to praying together; none of these get to the crux of what unites us as well as to the points of separation.

Vatican Council II gave us a number of reasons why the liturgy had to be reformed, some dealing with our own community, for example, "to intensify the daily growth of Catholics in Christian living," and others addressing this very important issue of openness to others, for example, "to nurture whatever can contribute to the unity of all who believe in Christ; and to strengthen those aspects of the Church which can help summon all of mankind into her embrace."

When members of the parish staff and liturgy committee plan for ecumenical (with other Christians) and interfaith (with non-Christians) worship services, there has to be much sensitivity and consultation to arrange satisfactorily such events.

Interfaith services. 94

95. When might we celebrate such services?

Thanksgiving services are quite popular in many areas. Such events, as well as Memorial Day and Independence Day commemorations, are important to participate in, but should not be considered as ultimate ecumenical efforts. These three days are often more than tinged with nationalism and do not focus on church unity. This is the special goal we seek during the well-established Week of Prayer for Christian Unity, when Christians are invited to make some special efforts to promote unity. The dates for this observance are in January.

Be creative.

Printed material is available each year from the Graymoor Fathers, but such resources should not limit your imagination or local adaptations. You will probably find several people in your parish, on the liturgy committee or elsewhere, who would be eager to plan and help carry out such a service. They would do well, depending upon the denominations invited, to build upon one or several of our liturgical treasures. The evening prayer of the church would be the best model for a very mixed congregation. A word service in the presence of the blessed sacrament, and concluding with Benediction, might be very powerful for people with a highly developed respect for sacraments, such as Episcopalians. A third possibility for stretching people's consciousness and emphasizing the emotional bonds that unite us, would be an introduction to and celebration of the stations of the cross. (If the stations seem out of place during the Week of Prayer, you might like to invite people over on a Friday during Lent.)

95

Appropriate times for celebrating.

124

96. It is obvious that our church building needs renovation. Where do we begin?

Like the clothes we wear or the car we buy or the residence we choose, the church buildings we use say something about us to others. They also subconsciously define and concretize our self-image. Because of this truth, and because of our need to unite realities and ideals in as many aspects of church life as possible, it is right and just that each church look critically at its church every once in awhile.

Our starting point today, after Vatican II, is that liturgy is the sacred work of the whole people of God—that all the baptized, not just the ordained, are called as a community to actively, fully, and consciously participate in divine worship. In other words, the people in the pews assemble to be participants, not observers. Therefore the pews and other things in church, and the way we arrange them, should help the people to participate. But do they in fact participate?

Work of the people.

Clergy need to provide information and leadership in this area because the average lay person does not have experience, education, or mental permission to think that the church he or she knows so well might be deficient in its liturgical ordering. Yet the fact is that many of our churches, with the traditional distinct divisions between priest and people, sanctuary and seating area, promote poor theology: they concretize a deficient self-image. Certainly we can appreciate every church as an affirmation of belief in the existence of God and in the presence of God's kingdom among us. But we can also be critical of the furnishings and the art, the substandard facilities and the outdated arrangements, if these elements are out of sync with theological reality.

Leadership.

It can comfort us (and all the people in the parish) to realize that theology as expressed through architecture has often undergone changes. Consider how ideas about God and worship must have been modified by the move from the house churches of the apostolic era to the great basilicas given to the church by Constantine. Think of the feeling you have as you enter a large cathedral with its awesome space, and compare this feeling to your experience of whatever smaller, brighter, more crescent-shaped churches you may know. It is right to appreciate our past and to admire our community's architectural glories, but it is also necessary to assert the present needs of our assemblies and to give concrete service to the liturgical theology of Vatican II.

Appreciate the past.

Live in the present.

Beginning a renovation project.

96

125

97. What should be the primary focal points in a church building?

The three primary architectural elements in a church building are the altar, the ambo, and the chair from which the celebrating priest presides.

The **altar.** When most of us grew up, altars were long and narrow. They were long to complement the proportions of the often elaborate reredos and to support the missal in its two positions. They were narrow to enable the priest to reach across to the tabernacle. These functions are not applicable today, and yet many continue to believe that this is what an altar should look like.

Here is what the Bishops' Committee on the Liturgy says about the altar:

> The altar, the holy table, should be the most noble, the most beautifully designed and constructed table the community can provide . . . it is never used as a table of convenience or as a resting place for papers, notes, cruets, or anything else . . . The altar is designed and constructed for the action of a community and the functioning of a single priest— not for concelebrants. The holy table, therefore, should not be elongated, but square or slightly rectangular.

The **ambo.** The second permanent and crucial focus is the ambo—what we often refer to as the pulpit. This is the one place for the reading of all the Scriptures, for the homily, and the intercessions. It should be substantial, prominent, permanent, and set in a complementary relationship to the altar.

A much less impressive stand—what we often call a lectern—can be placed (if it is necessary at all) away from the pulpit, and used by the cantor and the person making announcements. The subservient relationship, even the unnecessariness of it, should be evident in the design and portability of the lectern.

The **chair.** The third important focal point in the sanctuary is the chair from which the priest presides. It should be in harmony with the altar and ambo, and never in front of either one. The best place, if sight lines allow, would be toward the back of the sanctuary. Flanking chairs for deacons and servers are advisable.

Environment and Art in Catholic Worship (Washington, DC: United States Catholic Conference, 1978) nos. 71-72.

97 Primary focal points in the building.

98. What should an ideal church look like?

Because every church is different, there is no "ideal" church. Because sites are different, there is no one way to set up the interior. Nevertheless, a 1984 document from the Bishops' Conferences of England and Wales mentions six very important considerations:

- ease of access—adequate doors, ramps;
- ease of movement—for processions, for communion lines, for the handicapped;
- visibility—ability to see the liturgical actions without excessive distance, obstruction, or glare;
- audibility—ability to hear from every part of the church; amplifying equipment for the deaf; acoustical treatment to combat street noises;
- comfort—seating and kneeling positions that give enough support and space; adequate temperature, ventilation, light-levels; other amenities;
- adaptability—some seating should be removable for wheelchairs or for other needs.

When all is said and done, the reason we build or renovate a church is to have a suitable place for the people of God to assemble and celebrate the eucharist with dignity and grace. Starting from this reality that the assembly is the reason for the church being, we will also make the church suitable for other liturgical celebrations at which the assembly gathers, e.g., baptism, reconciliation, marriage, etc.

An important fact is that a church should be designed for the ordinary needs of the usual assembly. Church space should be planned for the regular Sunday-of-Ordinary-Time congregation.

Seating should be provided as close to the focus of activity as possible. People spontaneously arrange themselves around something they want to see. So too church seating should be arranged so that the whole grouping of priest and people are in close visual range of one another. Being visually aware of others, not having only backs of heads to look at, increases the sense of community and participation. Thus long rectangular spaces work against us; radial or amphitheater shaped seating supports interaction best.

The Parish Church: Principles of Liturgical Design and Reordering (London: Catholic Truth Society, 1984).

A place for the people.

A place for the assembly.

The ideal church building.

98

99. What is the difference between a pulpit and a lectern?

The pulpit (sometimes called the ambo) is the one approved place for proclaiming all the scripture readings, for the responsorial psalm, for the homily (unless the homilist wants to sit and preach, as Augustine often did, and as the General Instruction [no. 97] allows); it may also be used for the general intercessions.

The word "lectern" as found in the English translation of the General Instruction of the Roman Missal can cause problems for some people, since the word "pulpit" is often used to refer to the more dignified place of the scripture readings, with the word "lectern" describing the less dignified stand from which the announcements may be made and from which the singing may be led.

99 Pulpit and lectern.

100. Just how important is the environment for Sunday eucharist?

I am indebted to Fr. Anthony Eremito, a priest of the Archdiocese of New York and an expert on liturgical environment, for what follows.

Whether we are consciously aware of it or not, art and environment play a vital role whenever people gather to worship. We are affected by what we see and hear and touch. We are taught by the shape of our space. For example, we are likely to become more active if we sit up close or around the altar. We are tempted to be more uninvolved as we are allowed to be further away from the activity. Even though we know this, too many communities have accepted the status quo. A long nave with an altar far in the front is not helping people to achieve full participation.

Space affects what we do.

There are those who discount the impact of environment. Maybe we do get used to things that are not beautiful in order to survive; but no church should be ugly. When people see St. Peter's basilica, they recognize it as beautiful, and are indeed helped to pray.

It is not just the shape that matters. The appointments in the church have to be a priority: fresh flowers instead of artificial flowers, dignified and substantial vestments for clergy and servers, paschal candles that are not thin to begin with and stubby most of the year, seats that are comfortable, kneelers that are not torn, carpets that are presentable and vacuumed, statues that are not gaudy and/or misplaced, one single prominent pulpit for the proclamation of all the readings with, if really needed, a smaller lectern for cantors and for announcements, and above all, an altar that is beautiful, uncluttered, and not temporary.

Ambiance matters.

Even if all the major items for a beautiful worship space can be checked off, there will always be more to do about the ambiance of our churches. We are never going to engage all the senses of all our congregants, but this is a worthy goal. For example, we know how the brain stores the response to a stimulus like incense; it is an immediate and usually welcomed identification of where we are. Colors and textures of vestments and hangings, spot lighting and dimmers, quality audio systems and projection equipment, glass containers for the holy oils and a more visible place for them, musical selections appropriate for the seasons, the scent of pine at Advent, the sight of pussy-willows in Lent. These are just some of the possibilities to enhance the environment and to engage more fully and please the people who come to our Sunday eucharist.

Importance of environment.

100